CLARE OF ASSISI

Clare OF Assisi

A HEART FULL OF LOVE

ILIA DELIO, O.S.F.

ST. ANTHONY MESSENGER PRESS
Cincinnati, Ohio

Excerpts from *Francis of Assisi: Early Documents*, volumes 1, 2 and 3, edited by
Regis J. Armstrong, J.A. Wayne Hellmann and William J. Short, copyright ©1999 and
Clare of Assisi: Early Documents, edited and translated by Regis J. Armstrong, copyright
©1993 reprinted with permission of New City Press.

Scripture passages have been taken from *New Revised Standard Version Bible*, copyright
©1989 by the Division of Christian Education of the National Council of the Churches
of Christ in the U.S.A., and used by permission. All rights reserved.

Cover design by Jeanne Kortekamp
Cover image by Mark Balma
Book design by Mark Sullivan

LIBRARY OF CONGRESS CATALOGING-IN-PUBLICATION DATA

Delio, Ilia.
Clare of Assisi : a heart full of love / Ilia Delio.
p. cm.
Includes bibliographical references and index.
ISBN 978-0-86716-789-4 (pbk. : alk. paper) 1. Clare, of Assisi, Saint, 1194-1253. 2.
Christian women saints—Italy—Assisi—Biography. I. Title.

BX4700.C6D42 2007
271'.97302—dc22
[B]

2006033695

ISBN 978-0-86716-789-4

Published by St. Anthony Messenger Press.
28 W. Liberty St.
Cincinnati, OH 45202
www.AmericanCatholic.org

Printed in the United States of America.

Printed on acid-free paper.

07 08 09 10 5 4 3 2 1

Contents

Acknowledgments

I would like to thank the Poor Clare communities who invited me into their midst to share my thoughts on Clare. These communities include the Poor Clares of Duncan, British Columbia, the Poor Clares of Columbus, New Jersey and the Poor Clares of Cincinnati, Ohio, as well as the Holy Name Federation of Poor Clares. I would also like to thank Sr. Briege McKenna and her community in Ireland for taking the time to read through the text and offer comments. All of these women have shown me the example of Clare's hospitality, generosity and, most of all, what it means to live with a heart full of love. I am grateful, too, to Dr. Thelma Steiger and Steven Kluge, O.F.M., for their careful reading of the manuscript and helpful comments. They continue to be faithful companions on the journey. My students at the Washington Theological Union, especially Kenneth Harrington and Joanne Cahoon, have offered tremendous insights on Clare's mirror mysticism. Lisa Biedenbach, editorial director of books at St. Anthony Messenger Press, has been a great help and support in the publication process, and Mary Curran-Hackett, who has become my "friendly editor" at the press continues to be of invaluable assistance. To them and to all who have helped make this book possible, thank you.

Preface

It is a beautiful spring day. I have just finished reading Ilia's book on Clare. I hear myself saying: "Was not my heart burning within me?" Throughout this text, I found myself resonating and coming alive with the spirituality of a woman I have grown to know, Clare of Assisi. I could almost hear Clare saying to me: "You grasp it! It's all about love, a deep, burning love for Jesus crucified. Jesus crucified manifesting his deep love for us!" Clare knew we become what we love. She was a lover and she was a teacher. Throughout this book, we are being taught that to love is to become one with the other. Contemplation is allowing oneself to be transformed into the image of the one we love.

Clare tells us: "[A]s a poor virgin, / embrace the poor Christ."[1] Clare understood that to truly be able to know and embrace Jesus, one needs to be poor. Being poor does not necessarily mean that we are in need of material things. Ilia tells us that to be poor is to embrace our humanity and realize our need for God. Ironically, to need God is to begin to possess God. To possess God is to possess all. Clare and Francis grasped that to be poor is to have the greatest of riches. Poverty frees us from the selfishness that binds our lives and opens up for us the space to let God in. It frees us to "gaze upon"[2] Christ, to see with the eyes of our hearts, and when we see with "spiritual eyes" we find that we begin to see life and the world around us differently.

Ilia reminds us that for Clare, and for Francis also, contemplation is not an end in itself. Contemplation calls us beyond ourselves. Contemplation necessitates transformation. As we become one with Jesus, we are called to imitate him. Transformation asks us to give ourselves over to the one we love. In the Incarnation, Jesus taught us that there are no limits to God's love for us. Contemplation calls us to that same love. As we are transformed into the image of our God, we learn to love others as Jesus does. Such self-sacrificing love could really change our world. Forgiveness would replace retaliation. Dialogue would replace violence and war.

Lastly, I believe Ilia has captured the heart of Clare's eucharistic spirituality. Clare's hours in adoration taught her to know and to love her God. When in danger, she went straight to Christ in the Eucharist and asked his protection.[3] She was also willing to lay down her life for her sisters and the citizens of Assisi. Clare's time with God always led her to give herself for others. The humility of God gives us God's presence with us in a piece of bread and in the act of foot washing. We adore, we receive, we become. We become God for one another in our care, our service, and in all our acts of love.

Each one of us is a manifestation of God to one another. Our manifestation of God is uniquely ours. God dwells within each of us. Clare understood the reality of the Divine Indwelling. She passes that understanding down to us. As we make this understanding our own, our potential to see God present in all of God's creatures grows, and our reverence for all people becomes instinctive.

Our God is Trinitarian. The essence of who God is clearly is three divine persons in relationship. Prayer taught Clare how to live in relationship with all. Ilia passes this wisdom on to us. The unity of all creation is in God. We live in a world that hungers to make this reality our own. We desire to know the peace that such unity brings. Thank you, Clare of Assisi, for modeling the way. Thank you, Sr. Ilia, for exploring this way for us.

Sr. Claire Andre Gagliardi, O.S.C.
Monastery of St. Clare
Chesterfield, New Jersey
April 27, 2006

NOTES

[1] Clare of Assisi, "The Second Letter to Agnes of Prague," 82, in *Clare of Assisi: Early Documents*, Regis J. Armstrong, trans. (Saint Bonaventure, N.Y.: Franciscan Institute, 1993), p. 42.

[2] Clare of Assisi, "The Second Letter to Agnes of Prague," p. 42.

[3] Clare of Assisi, "The Acts of the Process of Canonization," p. 165.

Introduction

In every age a saint is born. Not that someone is born a saint but there is something about them, a characteristic or trait that distinguishes a person or, at least, marks one for life. Clare of Assisi is one such person. Born around 1194 to a wealthy family of nobility, the clan of Offreduccio, Clare was the first of three children. It is said that her mother was apprehensive of Clare's birth and went on pilgrimage to pray for her safe delivery. While she was at prayer one day she heard the words: "O Lady, do not be afraid for you will joyfully bring forth a clear light that will illumine the world." The word for *clear* in Italian is *chiara;* hence the name "Clare" or "bright one." Clare grew up in a household of holy women, including her mother, sisters and cousins. Poverty and penance were practiced at home among the women, and Clare gained a reputation for holiness at a young age. While she probably heard Francis of Assisi preach at the local church of San Rufino in 1208 or 1210, it is likely that her religious vocation was in place long before their encounter.

Clare was twelve years younger than Francis and met him around 1211 when she was seventeen. According to "The Acts of the Process of Canonization," Francis had already heard of Clare before their first meeting. It is unsure what the meetings between Francis and Clare involved but it is likely that he spoke to her about following Christ and living the gospel life. At about the age of eighteen, with the consent of Bishop Guido of Assisi, Clare decided to devote herself to a kind of penitential life closely linked to Francis and his brothers, whose form of life Pope Innocent III had approved orally only a few years before. On the night of Palm Sunday 1212, Clare ran away from home and was received into Francis' fraternity at the small church of the Portiuncula, below the town of Assisi in the Umbrian valley.[1]

The Italian scholar Maria Pia Alberzoni says that the beginning of religious life for Clare, as for Francis, was obscure since there was no clear path to follow. Apparently after Clare joined Francis and the brothers at the Portiuncula where Francis began his movement, Clare received the tonsure and dressed as a penitent. Francis then placed her in the monastery of San Paolo delle Abbadesse where she was received as a kind of servant, since she had given away her belongings to the poor and had no dowry to warrant entrance into the monastic community. The sources indicate that her family opposed her radical choice of life and tried to get her to abandon it, even by using force, but without success.[2] After some time, Clare moved to San Angelo in Panzo which was probably a house of penitents, where she was joined by her sister Catherine (who would be known in religious life as Agnes). Although their Uncle Monaldo tried to capture Catherine and bring her home, he was once again unsuccessful. Both Clare and Catherine eventually moved to the convent of San Damiano where they found a more permanent arrangement. This move shows the close affiliation of Clare to the movement of Francis. Neither her stay in the Benedictine monastery of San Paolo nor her stay among the penitents allowed her access to Francis and his brothers. However, a double community of brothers and sisters at San Damiano seemed a likely solution. Thus, as Alberzoni writes,

> Clare and Agnes established themselves at San Damiano, one of the places where the brothers were accustomed to stay when they were in the vicinity of Assisi. In fact, the new community always felt that it was part of the fraternity headed by Francis, which was made clear by their close relationship with the brothers living at San Damiano.[3]

Clare and her sister were joined by their mother and two cousins, and soon after many women followed. According to her *Rule*, Clare promised obedience to Francis and Francis promised care and solicitude for Clare and her sisters.[4] What unfolded, however, was the unpredictable involvement of the ecclesiastical hierarchy in this new, vibrant movement. The cardinal protector of the Franciscans, Hugolino (later known as Pope Gregory IX), did not approve of the rising number of women's communities (like Clare's) that were living independently and in poverty. He therefore decided to reform these women's communities in central Italy by bringing them into a unified system of monastic life. Clare's monastery of San Damiano became the umbrella for reform much to the dismay of Clare herself. Recent evidence has shown that Clare and her sisters were co-opted by Hugolino into the monastic reform while Francis and the friars began to distance themselves, probably due to internal divisions among their rapidly growing order.[5] What we know is that Clare and her sisters, also known as the "Poor Ladies," were caught up in a tangled web between the prelates of the church and the friars.

Although it is beyond the scope of this introduction to provide a detailed analysis of Hugolino's reform of religious life, it is worth noting that Clare and her sisters, while imposed upon with elements of monastic life, also held to their desire for Franciscan evangelical life, that is, a life dedicated to following the gospel of Jesus Christ. It is interesting that although Clare lived under a monastic rule for most of her life,[6] her spirituality does not characterize the classic monastic ascent to God. Whereas the monastic ascent is marked by a Neoplatonic structure in which the material world is transcended in pursuit of spiritual perfection, Clare emphasized the Incarnation as the starting point for union with God. The Neoplatonic ladder of ascent is a movement away from the world, rising above natural, sensible things as if they were inferior and in some sense, not truly real.[7] In this respect, the Neoplatonic tradition with its insistence on inner illumination and mental ascent diminishes the natural goodness of the created world which should motivate one to turn inward in the search for God. While both Clare and Francis left the world to pursue God insofar as they abandoned their status, wealth and security, never did they renounce the world for the sake of God. Rather, they realized that the created world was the world embraced by God; thus God could not be found apart from the world. The world, not the monastery, was the true cloister. It is not entirely clear whether or not Clare and her community in its early phase lived like the friars, following Christ in the world. Clare wanted a life like Francis: following the poor and humble Christ; sharing the life of the poor through manual labor; begging for food when necessary; attending to the suffering and poverty around her; and living a life of prayer and sympathy with all creation. The bishop of Acres, Jacques de Vitry, wrote an account of the "lesser brothers and sisters" while passing through the Umbrian valley in 1216. According to his account, these brothers and sisters

> ...went into the cities and villages during the day to preach the Gospel and give themselves to the active world; but they returned to their hermitages or solitary places at night, employing themselves in contemplation. The women lived near the cities in various hospices, accepting nothing but living from the work of their hands.[8]

Could these "lesser sisters" be Clare and her companions living a penitential life near the brothers? Such an arrangement may have been possible in the beginning of the movement, before enclosure was enforced on the Poor Ladies of San Damiano. Although she eventually had to assume the customs and enclosure of monastic life, it is evident that Clare never abandoned her heart's desire to follow the footsteps of Christ.

What exactly is this evangelical life that enkindled the hearts of Francis and Clare? Evangelical life is gospel life, a life centered on living the gospel, following the footsteps of Jesus Christ. It is not surprising that both Francis and Clare begin their rules by saying, "the form of life...is this: to observe the Holy Gospel of our Lord Jesus Christ."[9] In this way they indicated that evangelical life is centered neither on work nor ministry but on how we experience the presence of God through Christ. The foundation of evangelical life is the human person and the sharing among persons of the experience of Christ. The experience of God in the flesh emphasizes being a "person in relationship," that is, a brother or sister. This emphasis on encountering God incarnate as sister or brother distinguishes evangelical life from monastic or apostolic life. Because the human person is the fundamental focus, one can be anyplace or do anything within the framework of the gospel and still be a Franciscan because the form of Franciscan life is the form of the gospel. We might say that the primary purpose of evangelical life is to imitate Christ and to make that experience of Christ available to others.

One has only to examine Clare's spirituality (as we will do here) to realize that hers is a spirituality for evangelical life. Her Franciscan heart reveals itself in her writings which are grounded in the scandalous love of the crucified Spouse. Her language is not that of the soul in pursuit of a remote, transcendent God or of intellectual spiritual union. Rather, her two feet stand on a God-centered Earth and her eyes are fixed on the person of Jesus Christ and being a person in relationship. How did she attain an evangelical spirituality in a monastic milieu? I would suggest that Clare, like other medieval women under restricted conditions, focused inwardly on her deep desire for God. This deep desire, honed by years of reflection on the crucified Christ, unfolded within her. The opportunity to guide others in her way of life, such as Agnes of Prague, allowed her to express her ideas more freely or, we might say, to express the lines of love written on her heart.

It is not only her spirituality, however, that supports Clare's desire for evangelical life. Historically, there are two fundamental aspects of her life that suggest she fought tooth and nail for Franciscan evangelical life: the privilege of poverty and the *Rule*. The privilege of poverty was essential to Clare's way of life because it demanded a total dependence on the generosity and dedication of others for their well-being.[10] Pope Gregory IX, however, insisted that a mitigated form of poverty as found in the Benedictine and Augustinian expressions of religious life was better because it allowed a certain degree of ownership to secure the needs of the monastery. He imposed on the Poor Ladies of San Damiano a *Form of Life* based on the Benedictine Rule in order to provide a more stable form of life for them; however, two important points were missing: the pursuit of gospel poverty inspired by Francis and dependence on the Friars Minor.[11] Clare reacted intensely. At one point she threatened a hunger strike when the friars were prohibited from serving as preachers to the sisters.[12] Although the pope admired Clare and sought to provide security for her monastery, he eventually conceded and granted the privilege of poverty—but only to the Poor

Ladies of San Damiano and not to their sister monasteries. The privilege of poverty was again affirmed by Pope Innocent IV to Clare and her sisters upon promulgation of her *Rule (Solet Annure)*, which was approved by the pope the day before she died.

Clare had been the first woman in history to write her own rule for a community and have it approved; yet, it was not without immense struggle. The ecclesiastical intervention on the convent at San Damiano by Cardinal Hugolino was a source of constant tension for Clare. While Hugolino wanted to ensure protection and stability for the Poor Ladies of San Damiano, Clare and her sisters wanted to remain united to the inspiration of Francis and thus with the Friars Minor, reflected by their insistence on the privilege of poverty. Clare dealt effectively with the reform program of Hugolino and was able to mediate her way of life despite the pressure of monastic enclosure. Her own *Rule*, which she insisted on relentlessly, was approved by Pope Innocent IV in 1253 and contains the essence of her way of life, including the promise of Francis and the brothers to care for the sisters. Clare's *Rule* testifies to her fidelity to Francis and his way of life, indicating that she was indeed Franciscan.[13] Her entire religious life, however, was a struggle to see her *Rule* approved.

Even if one did not know Clare's historical background, one would surmise, based on her few writings, that she was a woman of firm conviction and strong will. She was, essentially, uncompromising in her desire to live the gospel life. Indeed, some scholars have wondered who exactly was responsible for the historic unfolding of the Franciscan movement and its spirituality. Did Clare's association with Francis give her a different start compared to other medieval women? Should she be regarded as a most faithful disciple of Francis but with a notion of fidelity that is static and imitative? Or should she be understood as uniquely responsible for the growth of the Franciscan vocation in the church during the twenty-seven years after the death of Francis in which she continued to govern, write and legislate? There is little doubt that Francis had in mind from the beginning that women would be involved in the mission of his order, and Clare responded to his search for a female collaborator.[14]

According to Thomas of Celano, Francis prophesied that San Damiano "would be a monastery of Christ's holy virgins."[15] According to hagiographical sources, it was Clare who led Francis to commit himself to an active life of preaching and service, when he might have preferred to remain a contemplative,[16] and it was Francis who convinced Clare to accept the restrictions on women's religious lives and the necessity for some kind of enclosure. In her *Rule* Clare described herself as "La Piantacella" ("the little plant" of Francis) connoting the deep affiliation she felt with him in his pursuit of gospel life. She preserved in her *Rule* the promise of Francis and his brothers to maintain care and solicitude for the sisters, a promise she held fast to as opposition from the friars mounted after Francis' death.

It is difficult to sort out the relationship between Francis and Clare. Although she is clearly faithful to his gospel way of life, she is more than just a faithful follower. Two stories show the close affinity (if not symbiotic relationship) between Francis and Clare. One story from the *Fioretti* recounts a meal they shared at the Portiuncula. The *cittadini*, the local inhabitants, saw the place in a blaze of fire and went to the Portiuncula only to find Francis, Clare and their companions rapt in a mutual ecstatic experience.[17]

The second is an account from Clare's "The Acts of the Process of Canonization" where three of the sisters (Filippa, Cecilia and Amata), all of whom were encouraged by Clare to join her, tell of a dream shared with them. Clare carried hot water to Francis who was standing at the top of a flight of stairs. When Clare reached Francis, she suckled at his breast and tasted sweet milk which she drank. Clare then bit Francis's nipple and held it between her lips. She then took the nipple in her hands and it became gold.[18] The Italian scholar Marco Bartoli has made a detailed analysis of this dream and notes that Clare relives with Francis that primitive experience of total rapport and affectivity.[19] The bite of the nipple represents the desire to take something that is other than ourselves in order to make it part of ourselves. Bartoli indicates that Clare's desire was not simply to make Francis her own, to possess him, but she desired a fuller identification—she wanted to become one with Francis. This notion of unity with Francis was not merely spiritual but physical (that is, sharing a way of life together) as well. The biographers indicate that to Francis, Clare was the true Christ, and to Clare, Francis was her pillar of strength, her support and consolation. It is likely that Clare represented Francis' ideal or at least embodied the essence of his ideals. Her spirituality indicates that she had an imprint of his soul on her heart and superimposed her own inner portrait onto his figure. She truly wanted to join with him and the brothers in their pursuit of the gospel life but was thwarted in her path. How united to Francis was Clare or how united to Clare was Francis? Where does one end and the other begin? There are no real answers to these questions, for each contributed to a movement that is masculine and feminine, active and contemplative, missionary and mystical. Francis and Clare form a coincidence of opposites centered in the person of Jesus Christ.

Although some see the first order (Friars) as the active, apostolic branch of order, and the second order (Clares) as the contemplative branch, this idea is found neither in the writings of Francis or Clare who proposed one and the same form of gospel life in imitation of Christ. It is no secret that Francis desired a life of prayer and contemplation. Did Clare fulfill Francis' ideal in her own way? Recent evidence tells us that Francis closely aligned himself to Clare and her sisters in the early years; however, as his movement grew and developed, sources indicate a growing distance. Alberzoni states, however, that while Francis distanced himself from the sisters as the movement grew, he gradually drew closer to them in the most critical moments of his final days, as death drew near.[20] Whatever transpired between Clare and Francis, we must conclude that the relationship between them remains an interesting, if ambiguous, one. Clare died twenty-seven years after Francis, on August 11, 1253, in the Assisi monastery where she had spent over forty years, surrounded by her sisters and two of Francis' first companions, Angelo and Leo. That neither the Minister General nor other brothers were present at her funeral suggests that

Clare remained a source of contention among the friars after Francis' death. Yet as Alberzoni notes, "her death marked the end of an era, since it meant the loss of a moral authority...that single handedly had defended the memory of Francis and the lifestyle shown by him."[21]

There are few writings on Clare, compared to the volumes on Francis, and Clare herself left only a handful of writings. Of what remains we have four letters to Agnes of Prague, a *Rule* and a Blessing that are authentically Clare's voice. The authenticity of the letter to Ermentrude of Bruges is questionable. The text known as her *Testament* was recently argued to be a fifteenth-century forgery produced by a convent in Florence seeking to reform,[22] although the ideas within the text reflect Clare's thought. Of these writings, it is the letters to Agnes of Prague that interest us because they contain the essence of Clare's ideas on the spiritual life. Although there are only four short works (as one friar exclaimed, "what can you say in four short letters?") they are rich in depth and meaning. I believe these letters contain the heart of Clare's spirituality which is centered on the Incarnation and transformation in Christ. Clare did not have a formal education (nor was there a library at San Damiano); thus her ideas are drawn from the liturgy, the Scriptures, her memory and a few good homilies from Cistercian monks and Franciscan friars. She relies heavily on the Gospel of Matthew and offers us a meditation on Matthew's theology of the kingdom possessed by those who are truly poor.[23] While there is no mention of her use of secretaries, there are reasons to conclude that she employed others to help her. Recent evidence has shown, for example, that Brother Leo was probably the scribe of Clare's fourth letter to Agnes, composed shortly before she died, after suffering years of illness.[24]

Since Clare's letters are written to the woman Agnes of Prague, a few words on Agnes are in order.[25] Like Clare, Agnes was born into nobility in 1205. Her father was King Premsyl Ottokar I of Bohemia and her mother, Queen Constance of the Hungarian Arpad dynasty. She was engaged at an early age to a son of the duke of Silesia and was sent to that court to live. Her education there was supervised by Queen (later saint) Hedwig. When Agnes was three years old, the young duke died so she returned to Prague and was placed in a Premonstratensian monastery for her education. Shortly after, she was engaged to the son of Emperor Frederick II, the future Henry VII, who was in residence at the court of Duke Leopold of Austria. Agnes was then sent to Austria to live, but after some time, she was jilted by the young Henry who married the duke's daughter. Agnes again returned to Prague where her angry father resolved to wage war against Leopold. However, Agnes persuaded him not to take revenge. She was eventually offered marriage by Frederick II (when his wife had died) but her father did not accept the offer. Agnes was therefore free to remain in Prague and devote herself to charitable works.

Around 1225 she met the Friars Minor who had recently arrived in the city. It is likely through the friars that she heard of Clare and the life of the Poor Ladies at San Damiano. The monastery in Prague that Agnes entered in 1234 was formed in 1233 by nuns coming from Trent. Upon entering the monastery, Agnes was immediately named abbess. In that same year, Agnes, knowing about the lifestyle observed at San Damiano, contacted Clare, expressing her desire to introduce in her community the form of life established by Francis for the religious women of Assisi. Pope Gregory IX was explicitly asked to authorize the change of Agnes's community into the "Clarian" direction which caused grave concern for the pope, since such approval would compromise the unity of his monastic reform.[26] Agnes, like Clare, had to endure papal restrictions on her way of life despite her resistance. Impelled to live under Gregory IX's form of life, Agnes and her sisters were ordered to follow the rule of Benedict until such time that a new rule for the Order of San Damiano was promulgated (1247) and reference to the rule of Benedict was eliminated.[27] Both Agnes and Clare had to fight for a way of life that was faithful to Francis.

Clare's first letter to Agnes is written in 1234, around the time when Agnes decided to embrace her new way of life. As we will see, this letter encapsulates Clare's understanding of poverty as she sees it rooted in God. This letter of spiritual depth would set the stage for

Clare's guidance of Agnes, even though they would never meet. Clare wrote to Agnes again in 1235 with an emphasis on contemplation of the poor crucified Christ. This theme is repeated and expanded in her next letter of 1238 in which Clare draws connections between contemplation, transformation and participation in the Body of Christ. The final letter is written fifteen years later in 1253, shortly before Clare's death. Here, at the end of her life, she reveals her deep love for Agnes, addressing the letter, "To her who is half of her soul and the special shrine of her heart's deepest love."[28] It is a beautiful letter that sums up Clare's spiritual path, the fulfillment of love in God and the journey into God.

Clare's spirituality does not develop systematically in her letters; rather, as we will see, it is like a finely stitched pattern on a soft, delicate cloth. One has to read her letters slowly and prayerfully, as she weaves her ideas into the pattern of Christ. Her path to God, however, can be summarized in four short ideas that she describes in her second letter to Agnes:

O most noble Queen,
gaze upon [Him],
consider [Him],
contemplate [Him],
as you desire to imitate [Him].[29]

While these four steps formed the basis of my book *Franciscan Prayer*, I explore them here more specifically in view of Clare's spirituality. These four basic themes—gaze, consider, contemplate, imitate—which characterize Clare's path to God, are the guiding lights of this book.

Having identified the pillars of Clare's thought, I must confess that the first chapter does not begin with the gaze but with the poverty of God. This is Clare's own starting point, as she describes the poverty of God in her first letter to Agnes. To expound Clare's thought I look at times to others, such as Francis and Bonaventure, whose spiritual writings are complementary to Clare's. In the first chapter, therefore, I examine the poverty of God in Clare's thought and then look to

Bonaventure's theology to seek the basis of the poverty of God based on Trinitarian relationships. While Clare emphasizes God as love, love is relational, and she frequently refers to the *persons* of the Trinity, as if experiencing God as a communion of persons in love. Her decisive focus on the crucified Christ leads us to explore the relationship between the Trinity and Christ. In this way, we come to a deeper understanding of the poverty of God who is love.

In the second chapter we continue on the theme of poverty but now the focus is on the human person. Here again Bonaventure and Francis help us to understand the depth of meaning that human poverty entails. Because poverty is Clare's desire, it is also the beginning of her path to God. Therefore, we explore the poverty of the human person and the gaze on the crucified Spouse as Clare describes this gaze in her letters to Agnes.

The object of the poor person who gazes forms the basis of the third chapter. Here Clare's novel idea of the mirror of the cross is introduced. The mirror of the cross is the crucified Christ and in the third chapter we explore in depth what it means to gaze into the mirror of the cross. We also begin to appreciate Clare's spirituality in its mystical dimensions. For the mirror of the cross, as she describes it, is the mirror image of our own human lives and the means of our transformation in God.

Chapter four explores the theme of the mirror but extends the self-reflective gaze into the notion of self, as the self strives for its true image and identity. Clare's path to God is not a series of discrete stages, rather it is more like interweaving strands of the Spirit. As the lover gazes on the beloved and comes to an acceptance of self in God, the self is transformed as an image of God. The bridge between self-acceptance and transformation is contemplation. Clare's path is a contemplative one but not in the sense of a world-denying vertical union, that is, union with God "above." Rather, contemplation for Clare is the fruit of gazing. It is the ability to see with the eye of the heart into the heart of God who is revealed in the crucified Christ. It is, we might say, a contemplation "from below." In this sense, contemplation is horizontally ecstatic, since one enters into union with God by way of vision.

In the fifth chapter we examine contemplation as the ability to see the depths of God hidden in the crucified Christ so that we may attain, like the beloved, the spirit of compassionate love. Seeing and loving are essential to Clare's spirituality. As we see so we love and, as we love, so we are transformed in love. Thus contemplation, as Clare describes it, is not the end of the spiritual journey but the center of it, the deepening of our relationship with God that ultimately impels us to be conformed to God and to be transformed in love.

Chapter six explores transformation as the becoming of one's true self in God, that is, becoming an image of God as God has created each one of us to be. The integral relationship between contemplation and transformation for Clare leads to the renewal of Christ's life in the believer. Transformation is examined in light of evangelical life. To be transformed is to imitate (or become the image of) Christ, and Clare sees the imitation of Christ as the enkindling of Christ's life in the world. She exhorts Agnes to pursue this goal and become a coworker with God, helping to build up the Body of Christ by becoming that body in her own life. It is at this stage of her spiritual path that we see Clare's tremendous contribution to Christian spirituality. Hers is a spirituality of participation and transformation. Unless we are poor enough and free enough to be transformed by love, the Body of Christ cannot grow; thus, both the church (which is the Body of Christ) and the world are diminished.

Clare strives for a eucharistic life, not necessarily receiving the Eucharist daily (which was not the practice of her time), but living like Christ, willing to give one's life for the sake of another. Chapter seven examines Clare's eucharistic spirituality in view of transcendent love, and looks to the example of Francis to see the implications of the Eucharist in view of one's own personal life.

Although Clare's spirituality is radically incarnational, one cannot deny the role of the Spirit in her thought. The Trinitarian patterns woven throughout her writings lead from the Father to the Son to the Spirit who is sent by Christ and conforms the human person to Christ.

Her movement into God is powered by the Spirit of love. It is a movement that is dynamic, forward in direction, light and swift, indicating
that life in God is not to be deterred by earthly matters. Highlighting
the role of the Spirit in Clare's letters allows us a glimpse into the
strength of her own life which, as we have briefly seen, was a series of
struggles. The Spirit, however, gave her power within. It imbued her
life with joy and freedom which can only come to one who lives deeply
in God. In chapter eight we look at the role of the Spirit in Clare's
thought and reflect on the relationship between the Spirit and Christ.
Looking at the relationship between the Spirit and Christ allows us to
come to new insight with regard to the work of the Spirit in our lives.
We find a new way of thinking about the Spirit in relation to Christ,
and we explore the role of the Spirit in view of the communion of saints
and the Body of Christ.

Although this is a small book on the spirituality of a medieval
woman, it is also a book about Christian life today. Clare's emphasis on
the person of Jesus Christ is an emphasis on the human person as well,
what we are and what we are called to be. Christ crucified is the mirror
in which we are to see our reflection, our strengths and weaknesses, our
failures and our capacity to love. Clare is not interested in the flight of
"the alone to the alone."[30] Rather, she asks, are you becoming a mirror
of Christ for others to see and follow? She wants us to reflect Christ in
our lives, to help build up the Body of Christ through transformation in
love, and to participate in the church. She is a mystic who calls us to
go forward into God by letting Christ take on our flesh so that we may
reflect the face of Christ to the world. She tells us not to be dissuaded
in the path to God, to be resolute in our convictions and trust the guidance of the Spirit in our lives. Clare, the woman who said "no" to the
pope and won his admiration, is a model for our time, for she shows the
strength of conviction in the face of opposition. Her thought is centered on the essence of human identity: Be yourself and allow God to
dwell within you. Christ will then be alive and the world will be created anew.

NOTES

[1] Maria Pia Alberzoni, *Clare of Assisi and the Poor Sisters in the Thirteenth Century*, William Short and Nancy Celaschi, trans. (Saint Bonaventure, N.Y.: Franciscan Institute, 2004), p. 10.

[2] Alberzoni, *Clare of Assisi and the Poor Sisters*, p. 10.

[3] Alberzoni, *Clare of Assisi and the Poor Sisters*, p. 11.

[4] "The Form of Life of Clare of Assisi", 6.1, in *Clare of Assisi: Early Documents*, Regis J. Armstrong, trans. (Saint Bonaventure, N.Y.: Franciscan Institute, 1993), p. 71. Hereafter referred to as *Early Documents*. A new edition of Clare's writings edited by Armstrong is scheduled to be published by New City Press in 2006. Clare writes: "After the Most High Heavenly Father saw fit by His grace to enlighten my heart to do penance according to the example and teaching of our most blessed Father, Saint Francis, I, together with my sisters, willingly promised him obedience shortly after his own conversion." The critical edition of Clare's writings are found in *Claire d'Assise: Écrits*, Marie-France Becker, Jean-François Godet and Thaddée Matura, eds., *Sources Chrétiennes*, no. 325 (Paris: Les Éditions du Cerf, 1985).

[5] For the history of the Poor Ladies see Maria Pia Alberzoni, "Clare of Assisi and Women's Franciscanism," Ed Hagman, trans. *Greyfriars Review* 17.1 (2003), pp. 5–38; Roberto Rusconi, "The Spread of Women's Franciscanism in the Thirteenth Century," Ed Hagman, trans., *Greyfriars Review* 12.1 (1998), pp. 35–75; Clara Gennaro, "Clare, Agnes and the First Sisters: From the 'Pauperes Dominae' of San Damiano to the Poor Clares," Ed Hagman, trans., *Greyfriars Review* 9.3 (1995), pp. 259–276.

[6] Regis Armstrong in his 1993 edition of the *Early Documents* of Clare states that "in order to provide a more stable form of living for the Poor Ladies . . . Hugolino gave them a new, detailed, and austere Form of Life based on the Benedictine Rule" (p. 22). He goes on to indicate the difficulties of this rule for Clare. Elizabeth Petroff states that "Clare had to accept more and more limitations on the heroic ideal of service she had initially chosen, until finally the rule she was given by the Pope was, in all essentials, that of the Benedictines. . . . It is no wonder that Saint Clare received this Rule with "amazement and affliction of soul" (See Elizabeth Petroff, *Body and Soul: Essays on Medieval Women and Mysticism* [New York: Oxford Unitversity Pess, 1994], pp. 26-27.) While these older sources indicate that Clare and her sisters lived under the Benedictine Rule, Alberzoni discusses the complexities of the form of life given to Clare due to papal intervention in her way of life. Hugolino's monastic reform used the San Damiano convent as the umbrella for the reform of women's religious life in central Italy. The origins of the order of San Damiano, Alberzoni claims, can be credited to the work of Hugolino and his desire to give the new order he founded a somewhat centralized structure along the lines of "tried and true monastic experience." "Such motives," she writes, "have led some to believe that the Cardinal of Ostia wanted to promote a reform within the Benedictine Order, but a reform no longer connected with the Cistercian men's monasteries which had decided to no longer

accept responsibility for the cura monialium" (p. 36). Although San Damiano was incorporated into the circle of Hugolinian monasteries, the pope had to confirm its "Franciscan" and "Clarian" distinctiveness which he did by granting the Privilege of Poverty in September 1228 (Alberzoni, "Clare of Assisi and Women's Franciscanism" p. 16). In the rule of 1247 given to the order of San Damiano (by Gregory IX), reference to the rule of Saint Benedict was removed but this really pertained only to observance of the three vows of poverty, chastity and obedience.

[7] Sean Edward Kinsella, "How Great a Gladness: Some Thoughts on Francis of Assisi and the Natural World," *Studies in Spirituality* 12 (2002), p. 66. According to Plato's "Allegory of the Cave," which was very influential on the structure of Neoplatonism, sensible reality is comprised of ersatz forms while the true forms lie in a transcendent, spiritual world.

[8] Jacques de Vitry, cited in Elizabeth Petroff, *Consolation of the Blessed* (New York: Alta Gaia Society, 1979), p. 26. According to Alberzoni, the lesser sisters "mentioned by Jacques de Vitry in 1216 should not in any way be traced back univocally to the experience of Clare and her first sisters, at that time only four years at San Damiano, and still living what we might call a penitential phase; this fact makes them similar to, and therefore difficult to distinguish from, many groups of the same time, widespread particularly in the Tuscan-Umbrian region." See Alberzoni, *Clare of Assisi and the Poor Sisters*, pp. 115–116.

[9] "The Form of Life of Clare of Assisi," 1.1 (*Écrits*, 124). *Early Documents*, p. 64. See also Francis of Assisi, "The Earlier Rule," 1.1 in *Francis of Assisi: Early Documents*, volume 1, *The Saint*, Regis J. Armstrong, J.A. Wayne Hellmann and William J. Short, eds. (New York: New City Press, 1999), p. 63. (Hereafter referred to as *FA:ED I* followed by page number.)

[10] Alberzoni, *Clare of Assisi and the Poor Sisters*, p. 23.

[11] Armstrong, *Early Documents*, p. 22.

[12] Leslie Knox, "Audacious Nuns: Institutionalizing the Franciscan Order of Saint Clare," *Greyfriars Review* 16.2 (2002), p. 160.

[13] It is worth noting Alberzoni's comment about the use of the word *Franciscan* as applied to Clare and her sisters. She writes: "It is therefore totally incorrect to speak of an "Order of Saint Clare" or "Poor Clares" before 1263, when that terminology was first officially used to designate the composite order which still contained diverse elements which the Apostolic See had made so many efforts to unify from the time of the pontificate of Gregory IX onwards. The sometimes indiscriminate use of such terminology has given rise to considerable misunderstandings causing people to see as "Franciscan" from its very beginning something that, at least initially, was not so" (*Clare of Assisi and the Poor Sisters*, pp. 31–32). Of course Alberzoni is writing as historian and within historiographical context. I think Clare's own writings, especially her letters, point to a decisively Franciscan stance despite the papal efforts to monasticize her way of life. I do think Clare is Franciscan from beginning to end, but from historical perspective other factors impinge on the use of this terminology.

14 It should be also noted, however, that while Francis' affection and respect for Clare was great, he was not interested in organizing or directing an order of enclosed women. Leslie Knox writes, "when his female followers included only Clare and her companions, he saw no reason that the friars and nuns should not have a close relationship. Yet as his frustration grew over his order's rapid growth and its shift away from his apostolic ideals, Francis withdrew from this position." Eventually he tried to keep the men and women completely separate and complained about the friars' obligation to the convents of nuns. See Knox, "Audacious Nuns," p. 158.

15 "The Remembrance of the Desire of a Soul by Thomas of Celano," 8 in *Francis of Assisi: Early Documents*, volume 2, *The Founder*, Regis J. Armstrong, J.A. Wayne Hellmann and William J. Short, eds. (New York: New City Press, 2000), p. 252. (Hereafter referred to as *FA:ED II* followed by page number.)

16 See Bonaventure, "The Major Legend of Saint Francis," 12.2 in *FA:ED II*, p. 623. According to Bonaventure, Francis felt called to preach the gospel but had to discern whether or not this was the right way. Thus "he also asked the holy virgin Clare to consult with the purest and simplest of the virgins living under her rule, and to pray herself with the other sisters in order to seek *the Lord's will* in this matter."

17 The description of this account is given in "The Little Flowers of Saint Francis," 15, in *Francis of Assisi: Early Documents*, volume 3, *The Prophet*, Regis J. Armstrong, J.A. Wayne Hellmann and William J. Short, eds. (New York: New City Press, 2001), pp. 590–591.

18 See Third Witness, "The Acts of the Process of Canonization," 29, in Armstrong, *Early Documents*, p. 152.

19 Marco Bartoli, *Clare of Assisi*, Sister Frances Teresa, trans. (Quincy, Ill.: Franciscan Press, 1993), p. 146.

20 Alberzoni, *Clare of Assisi and the Poor Sisters*, p. 25.

21 Alberzoni, *Clare of Assisi and the Poor Sisters*, p. 25.

22 Recent scholarship on the *Testament* of Clare indicates that this may not be an authentic work but rather belongs to the manuscripts of fifteenth century Poor Clares associated with the Observant Reform. W. Maleczek ("Das Privilegium paupertatis Innocenz III. Und das Testament der Klara von Assisi. Überlegungen zur Frage inhrer Echtheit," in *Collectanea Franciscana* 65 (1995), pp. 5–82) claims that the insistence on poverty in the *Testament* is more appropriate to the time of the Observant Reform in the second half of the fifteenth century than to the years before Clare's death (78). See translation by Cyprian Rosen and Dawn Nothwehr, "Questions About the Authenticity of the Privilege of Poverty of Innocent III and of the Testament of Clare of Assisi," *Greyfriars Review* 12 (Supplement, 1998), pp. 1–80. Although the *Testament* may be a forgery, as Maleczek contends, the principal points of the *Testament* follow Clare's thought as outlined in her letters to Agnes.

23 Armstrong, *Early Documents*, pp. 25–26

24 Timothy J. Johnson, "Clare, Leo, and the Authorship of the Fourth Letter to

Agnes of Prague," *Franciscan Studies* 62 (2004), pp. 91–100.

[25] For an introduction to Agnes's life see Armstrong, *Early Documents*, pp. 33–34.

[26] Alberzoni, *Clare of Assisi and the Poor Sisters*, p. 175.

[27] Alberzoni, *Clare of Assisi and the Poor Sisters*, pp. 179–180.

[28] Clare of Assisi, "The Fourth Letter to Agnes of Prague," *Early Documents*, p. 49.

[29] Clare of Assisi, "The Second Letter to Agnes of Prague," *Early Documents*, p. 42.

[30] This is the famous saying of the third-century Neoplatonist Plotinus. See Andrew Louth, "Plotinus" in *The Origins of the Christian Mystical Tradition: From Plato to Denys* (Oxford: Clarendon, 1981), p. 51.

Chapter One

THE POVERTY OF GOD

It is rare that we speak to one another about the poverty of God. Usually when we encourage one another in the pursuit of God, we describe positive attributes of God such as power, wisdom, mercy and kindness. The poverty of God seldom enters into the conversation because poverty seems so "unnatural" to God. Yet, it is "God-centered" poverty that absorbs Clare's attention in her first letter to Agnes. Here, in a short paragraph of rare depth, Clare indicates why poverty is essential to the pursuit of God—because poverty is the expression of love. She writes:

> O blessed poverty,
>> who bestows eternal riches
>>> on those who love and embrace her!

> O holy poverty,
>> God promises the kingdom of heaven
>>> and, in fact, offers eternal glory and a blessed life
>>> to those who possess and desire you!

> O God-centered poverty,
> whom the Lord Jesus Christ
>> Who ruled and now rules heaven and earth,
>> Who spoke and things were made,
>>> condescended to embrace before all else![1]

For Clare, poverty is the foundation of life in God because poverty begins with God. To identify poverty in relationship to God is to quickly dispel the notion of poverty as merely material want or need.

Clare realized that the accumulation of material things can stand in the way of God and she sought to dispossess herself of things. However, the God-centered poverty that she highlights is more than material dispossession. Poverty touches upon the very basis of existence itself, the gift of God given to us in the person of Jesus Christ. The poverty of God according to Clare is identified with the Incarnation, and because the Incarnation is the person of Jesus Christ, we can claim that the poverty of God is expressed vis-à-vis the human person. In her first letter to Agnes, Clare puts forth the tremendous mystery of the human person both as rich and poor, a mystery which she will expound in her subsequent letters. The mystery can be stated in this way: We are rich in our poverty but we must possess poverty to know our wealth in God. Clare does not see the meaning of poverty as living in deprivation but living fulfilled in God. Her understanding of poverty is paradoxical. To embrace poverty is to be endowed with riches; to possess and desire poverty is to receive God's promise of the kingdom of heaven. The poor person is not the one in need of material things but the one in need of God and the one who needs God possesses God and to possess God is to possess all.

Clare's insight to the poverty of God is the visible expression of self-gift which she sees in the crucified Christ. She writes:

> O God-centered poverty,
> whom the Lord Jesus Christ
>> Who ruled and now rules heaven and earth,
>> Who spoke and things were made,
>> condescended to embrace before all else![2]

For Clare, the one who rules from the tree of the cross lived his earthly life poor and on alms to reveal to us the goodness of God. On the cross that same goodness is shown to us in the outstretched arms of the Crucified. The poverty of the crucified Christ is essential to Clare's spirituality because it speaks to her of the human capacity for greatness and also the capacity for weakness—what we are and what we are called to be. Christ is the human person *par excellence* not because he is perfect or without sin or even because he is God. Rather Christ is the human person *par excellence* because of the totality of his love; he reveals to us the human capacity to love. Poverty is the language of love.

Clare is a mystic who delights in living in the mystery of God. She assures Agnes that God has invited her into the divine embrace if she is willing to accept the invitation. As she enters into that embrace, she is to realize the transience of earthly things and the infinite wealth of heaven, which is not a place but a relationship of love. In the cross of Jesus Christ, Clare realizes that God does not hold back anything for himself but rather gives himself completely to us. Divine revelation is the movement of God to poverty. The One who is rich in love comes down to where we are, takes on our humanity, and extends his arms on the cross to embrace us in love. In the mystery of the cross, therefore, Clare sees that God is self-giving and self-gift. God gives everything to us in the gift of the Son or, in Clare's words, the "beloved Spouse." God loves us to such a degree we might say that God "throws it all away" out of love to be God-for-us. The poverty of God is the source of our true riches because "God promises the kingdom of heaven to those who possess and desire you [poverty]."[3] The sign of God's outpouring love is the cross which manifests to Clare the victory of love. She tells Agnes that she is already caught up in God's embrace[4] (of love), indicating that God does not love us for what we do but for who we are. God does not love us because we are good or perfect or do nice things but simply because God is love. Love is what God does because God is love. Those who "desire and possess" poverty, Clare indicates, live in the embrace of God's love.

Clare's thought is deceptively simple because it is centered on the mystery of God's love in the paradox of the cross. Her relationship to the crucified Christ is *theo*-logical because her understanding of God filters through the "logic of the cross." It is not a rational understanding of God, a deduction of insight based on certain premises. Rather, one might say that, for Clare, relationship to God is living in paradox because in the mystery of the cross Clare finds the key to life. The key to the door of life, is a mystery of opposites: death/life, poverty/riches, contempt of the world/spiritual joy, earth/heaven, time/eternity, goods of the earth/things of heaven. In her first letter to Agnes, for example, she writes:

> [S]ince contempt of the world has pleased You more than its honors, poverty more than earthly riches, and You have sought to store up greater treasures in heaven rather than on earth.... Your reward is very rich in heaven! (Mt 5:12).
>
> ...
>
> What a great and praiseworthy exchange:
> to leave the things of time for those of eternity,
> to choose the things of heaven for the goods of the earth,
> to receive the hundred-fold in place of one,
> and *to possess* a blessed eternal *life!*[5]

In her own remarkable way, Clare understands the mystery of the Incarnation through spiritual insight. She does not try to "explain" the cross to Agnes. Rather, she indicates that the crucified Christ reveals to us the God of love who has taken on our humanity, lived in poverty and died on a cross. He is our path to life, the source of our happiness and joy and our assured passage to heaven—not because the cross is like a train that takes us to a place called "heaven" but because heaven is an unimaginable relationship with God in love.

Clare's description of "God-centered" poverty is written with conviction and assurance, as if Clare had a glimmer of that glory which the human eye cannot see, especially embodied in the strange figure of the cross. From where did her assurance come? The simplest answer is faith, as the author of the Letter to the Hebrews writes: "Now faith is the assurance of things hoped for, the conviction of things not seen" (Hebrews 11:1). How does one come to this deep level of faith? Spending time with God. One can only surmise that Clare spent many hours dwelling on the mystery of God, ruminating on the mystery within her and striving to live in the mystery, as she went about her daily life. Having surrendered wealth, nobility and aristocracy—a life of comfort and leisure—it is likely that Clare, like Agnes, would not settle for anything less than a life totally dedicated to God. The cross convinced her that God has totally given himself to us; thus, it is only reasonable that we should give ourselves totally to God. For Clare, there seems to be nothing in between—neither mediocrity nor compromised self-gift. The God who has given himself to us in the poverty of the cross is the God who claims us as his own.

Clare is a mystic who dwells in love. While there are all types of mystic "dwellers" Clare is focused on the Incarnation as the wellspring of love. The fullness of God's love has been poured out in Jesus Christ. The poverty of God is the fullness of Jesus Christ; the poverty of Jesus Christ is the fullness of God. Because Clare's ideas are scattered about ever so briefly in her letters, one must look to other Franciscan writers to gain insight into her notion of the poverty of God who is love. The great theologian Bonaventure of Bagnoregio indicated that love does not exist in isolation; rather, love goes out to another to unite with another. Love therefore requires a lover and a beloved and, if it is to be perfect, a co-beloved.[6] The Trinity is perfect love because it is a communion of divine persons-in-love.

To speak of God as a Trinity of persons-in-love is to realize that God is relational. Relationship is not something tacked on to God when God gets lonely and wants some company. God does not "will" relationship by sheer decision. Rather, God is an endless ocean of love, a community of lovers united to one another in a perfect union of love; a society of lovers, mutually in-dwelling in the justice that is love; a family of lovers, each with a personality distinct from the other precisely because union in love differentiates. The uniqueness of each person is the basis of union. To speak of God as love is to realize that isolation and autonomy have nothing to do with God. Everything that exists is intended for relationship, and the multiplicity of things that exist—plurality—is never meant to be a collection of individual things but a unity of all things in love. Plurality and diversity reflect the mystery of God because God is a fecundity of love, an inexhaustible fountain of love that flows from the Father to the Son in the Spirit. The Father is the overflowing fountain of love who, by nature, shares love diffusively with another person, the Son, and the two persons are in such a deep, intimate bond of love that they breathe forth love in a single breath and this is the Spirit. Lover, beloved, co-beloved—such is our God who is Trinity.

In thinking about the mystery of the Trinity, Bonaventure wrote that the Trinity is marked by a type of love that is dynamic and inexhaustible. Love within the Trinity is always going out to another for the sake of the other. When we say that God is love, we are saying that God is personal and relational because by the very nature of being love, God is other-centered. The Father, the fountain fullness of love, is always moving toward the Son in the sharing of love, and the Son in turn loves the Father. The love between the Father and Son is so complete that it expresses itself in the person of the Spirit. The perfection of love requires not only a lover and a co-lover, therefore, but the fruit of their love must be expressed in another so that the perfection of love is always marked by self-gift.

I imagine the love of the Trinity not as static persons in relationship but like a harmony of energy between persons, ebb-and-flow relationships of love between the divine persons that are reflected in the energy forces of the universe. The love of the Trinity is not a series of "acts" or relationships of "give and take." Rather, it is one continuous act of love, a flow of love from the Father to the Son in the Spirit. This flow of love is an emptying forth from one person to the other which is renewed in the flowing back or return of love. Because love is dynamic and flows from one person to the other, it speaks to us of emptiness and fullness. The Trinity is three unique persons, each with their own "personality" and distinction, who act together in one single movement of harmony, unity and love. Although the Father is an infinite fountain of love, according to Bonaventure, the very communication of love to another, the Son, entails a type of emptiness or poverty. The poverty of the Father, we might say, is the eternal generation of the Son because it is in the self-emptying love of the Father that the Son is eternally begotten. The Father or first person of the Trinity is marked by emptiness and fullness. It is the fullness of the Father as the fountain source of love that enables the Father to share love totally with another without diminishment. The Son is the fruit of the Father's love because he is the fruit of the Father's overflowing goodness. Although the Father is an infinite fountain of love, the very communication of love to another, the Son, entails a type of poverty or emptiness. The poverty of the Father is marked by openness to the divine other which is expressed in the eternal generation of the Son. If the Father was not self-communicative love by nature, the Son would not *be*. The fullness of the Father would then be a self-contained autonomous one, and the Trinity would not exist. Instead the poverty of the Father is the basis of the poverty of God because the gift of the Father's love is the basis of the Trinity. Since the gift of love and the receptivity of love require openness or, we might say, emptiness, poverty is the underlying key to the mystery of God because poverty is that openness to love. In the ebb and flow of love's fecundity, the plurality of divine persons are united as one. God's poverty, therefore, is the basis of Trinitarian communion in that the Father's self-diffusive goodness, a goodness given totally, generously and freely, is the source of the Son and Spirit. The Trinity is not a self-sufficient and static community of persons but an interrelated and dynamic community of persons-in-love whose love is *given*, *received* and *shared*. It is the poverty of the Father, the dialectic of the Father's fountain fullness of goodness, that renders the Trinity an infinitely fecund community of divine life.

How do we make sense of the Trinitarian communion of love in our own lives? How does the Trinity of love relate to the crucified Christ? Clare does not address these questions but the seeds of her thought invite us to speculate on the significance of the human person. It is the human person, I believe, that enables Clare to contemplate the mystery of God. She is not an abstract thinker nor does she separate the mystery of Trinitarian love from the created world. Rather the person of Jesus Christ allows her to dwell on the capacity of the human person for God; and the capacity of God to unite with a human person enables her to consider the mystery of God as love. Indeed, if we were to juxtapose her first and fourth letters to Agnes we would see this

God-human relationship is the thread of her spirituality. While the first letter describes the God of love who enters into relationship with us, the fourth letter describes what we become when we enter into relationship with God. The crucified spouse is the center of freedom and transformation. We are invited into relationship by a God of self-giving love. When we respond to this invitation, we enter into the great mystery of God by entering into the great mystery of our own created being as persons who can reflect the image of God. To know God is to know the human person since the mystery of God *is* the human person. Clare's focus on the person of Jesus Christ was not simply devotional. In the life, death and resurrection of Jesus Christ she saw the nobility of the human person. She perceived that when we come to live in God and allow God to live in us, Incarnation is renewed. Every act of the human person then becomes an act of God insofar as God's love and the person's love become one in will and desire.

The poverty of God, seen in the cross, is an invitation to enter into the great mystery of God's love. Just as the cross signifies the drama of God's involvement with us, so, too, we are called into the drama of transformation in Christ. Poverty is not only the starting point of relationship with God but it is the deepening of poverty that enables the seeker to enter more deeply into the mystery of God. How one comes to this level of poverty that leads to transforming love is the genius of Clare's spiritual insight.

QUESTIONS FOR REFLECTION

1. How does God's love make a difference in your life?
2. How do you understand the Trinity as a community of love? Does the Trinity help shape your life in the everyday world?
3. What is significant about the poverty of God for you? Do you relate the poverty of God as love to the person of Jesus Christ?
4. How does God's love diffuse through you to others?

NOTES

[1] Clare of Assisi, "The First Letter to Agnes of Prague," 15–17 (*Écrits*, 86), *Early Documents*, p. 36.

[2] Clare of Assisi, "The First Letter to Agnes of Prague," 17 (*Écrits*, 86), *Early Documents*, p. 36.

[3] Clare of Assisi, "The First Letter to Agnes of Prague," 16 (*Écrits*, 86), *Early Documents*, p. 36.

[4] Clare of Assisi, "The First Letter to Agnes of Prague," 10 (*Écrits*, 84), *Early Documents*, p. 35.

[5] Clare of Assisi, "The First Letter to Agnes of Prague," 22, 30 (*Écrits*, 88–90), *Early Documents*, pp. 37–38.

[6] For a discussion on love and the Trinity in Bonaventure see Ilia Delio, *Simply Bonaventure: An Introduction to His Life, Thought and Writings* (New York: New City Press, 2001), pp. 39–53.

Chapter Two

THE POVERTY OF BEING HUMAN

We read daily in the newspaper about poverty around the world. Sometimes the stories are directly beneath the stock market quotes or surrounded by stories of the world's wealthiest people. The juxtaposition may be coincidental or purposeful. I tend to think the latter is true because poverty makes us nervous.

The unnerving quality of poverty makes Clare's emphasis on poverty difficult to grasp. Her desire to be poor, however, was not a glorification of human deprivation or neglect but her desire for God. Had she not beheld the poverty of God as the immensity of divine love, I wonder if she would have pursued a life of poverty so vigorously or urged Agnes to do so. In her first letter to Agnes she writes: "You have rejected all these things and have chosen with Your whole heart and soul a life of holy poverty and destitution."[1] It is difficult to understand how a woman of the aristocracy could choose a life of poverty and destitution and be happy, unless she had an understanding of poverty beyond material means. Clare had a God-centered understanding of poverty. For Clare, the logic of poverty was the logic of love. She saw the poverty of God as the fountain fullness of love, the love that brings us into being, sustains us and yearns for us. Her emphasis on the centrality of love is characteristic of Franciscan spirituality in general. We are created out of love, in love and for love, as the Spanish mystic Ramon Llull wrote:

> They asked the Lover where he was from. He replied, "From love." "What are you made of?" "Love." "Who conceived you?" "Love." "Where were you born?" "In love." "Who raised you?" "Love." "What do you live on?" "Love." "What is your name?" "Love." "Where do you

come from?" "Love." "Where are you going?" "To love." "Where are you?" "In love." "Do you have anything besides love?" He replied: "Yes, sins and offenses against my Beloved." "Does your Beloved pardon you?" The Lover said there was were mercy and justice in his Beloved and so he found shelter between fear and hope.[2]

How do we center ourselves in the love of God? Clare's answer is simple and disarming: Become poor. Clare wrote to encourage Agnes to pursue a life of poverty, to become poor enough to embrace the poor Spouse. It is hard to admit in a consumer culture that poverty is the key to the fullness of life. To the secular mind it seems absurd. Western culture is immersed in a capitalism based on the idea that worldly success is a blessing of God. The type of poverty that Clare and the Franciscans speak of is opposed to the spirit of capitalism and self-sufficency. It means to be dependent on others. That is exactly what Clare and Francis saw in the mystery of Jesus Christ. In his *Earlier Rule* Francis writes: "They must rejoice when they live...among the poor and the powerless.... Let them...remember, moreover, that our Lord Jesus Christ...was not ashamed. He was poor and a stranger and lived on alms."[3] Likewise, Bonaventure's "Commentary on the Gospel of Luke" highlights the poverty of Christ: "Remember how generous the Lord Jesus was: he was rich, but he became poor for your sake, to make you rich out of his poverty" (See 2 Corinthians 8:9).[4] Both Francis and Bonaventure perceived that Christ lived dependent on others so that God's goodness could be revealed. When we allow others to do things for us, God's goodness shines through them. Poverty is not so much about want or need; it is about relationship. Poverty impels us to reflect on our lives in the world from the position of weakness, dependency and vulnerability. It impels us to empty our pockets—not of money— but the pockets of our hearts, minds, wills—those places where we store up things for ourselves and isolate ourselves from real relationship with others. Poverty calls us to be vulnerable, open and receptive to others, to allow others into our lives and to be free enough to enter into the lives of others. While Clare (and Francis) call us to be poor so that we may enter into relationship with the poor Christ, they also ask us to be poor so as to enter into relationship with our poor brothers and sisters in whom Christ lives.

In her second letter to Agnes, Clare writes that she is to "gaze upon him [Christ]." Although she does not explicitly link poverty and gazing upon Christ, the foundation of poverty in her first letter and the call to "gaze upon him" in her second letter suggests that poverty is the basis of spiritual vision or contemplation. To gaze is not simply to see but it is to see with the eyes of the heart. It is the vision of the spiritually poor person who is inwardly free to contemplate the presence of God. If we are to enter into real relationship with God, we must become poor; we must embrace our poverty.

Economic poverty is not difficult to attain. Spiritual poverty, however, can be. It means relinquishing that which we possess to smother the ego or barricade it against the intrusion of others. It is the antidote to human violence, to the need to assert ourselves over and against others. Gazing upon the poor crucified Christ gave Clare insight into the human person. She realized that becoming poor is not contrary to the fulfillment of human nature but rather the very fulfillment of our humanity. Christ reveals to us that the human person is poor by nature. Our poverty however, is a forgotten poverty because the sin of self-centeredness has made us "grabbers" and "graspers." That is why conversion is the movement toward poverty because poverty is the basis of authentic humanity. To be a truly human person is to be poor. The poverty of the human person is not economic poverty but ontological poverty, the poverty of being human. Poverty means that human life, from birth to death, hangs on the threads of God's gracious love. While we may enjoy a wealth of goodness today, we may lose that wealth tomorrow. Life is radically contingent; nothing has to be the way it is. Everything is gift. In "The Sacrament of Creation" Michael and Kenneth Himes lift poverty from the margins of economic deprivation and place it directly in the center of the human condition, not as a definition but as a description. They write:

> The discovery of one's finiteness is the recognition of one's poverty.
> When one grasps the "iffiness" of one's existence, the shocking fact

that the source and foundation of one's being is not in oneself, then one knows oneself as truly poor.[5]

Many people know they are finite. Few, however, will admit they are poor. To say that I am poor is not to confess that I am without money or material things but that I am dependent on another, first, for the source of my own existence and then for every breath of air I breathe at each moment of time. My poverty says to me that I do not have to exist at all. I am here in this place at this time but it could have been different or otherwise. I may never have existed or I may have existed in another place at another time. The very fact that I am here is more than mere chance or coincidence. I am here not because I choose to be here (as if I could have chosen otherwise). I am here because it is God's will (which is really God's love) that has brought me into being. It is God's love that sustains my life for his love is the source of my life. If I could come to know this love then I could embrace my poverty and realize that in this poverty I am free to give glory to God. I would realize that my life comes from another and I am radically dependent on another, on God and on God enfleshed in other people, and in creation. Thomas Merton captured the poverty of the human person as the freedom of living in God's will when he wrote:

> For it is God's love that warms me in the sun and God's love that sends the cold rain. It is God's love that feeds me in the bread I eat and God that feeds me also by hunger and fasting. It is the love of God that sends the winter days when I am cold and sick, and the hot summer when I labor and my clothes are full of sweat....
>
> It is God's love that speaks to me in the birds and streams; but also behind the clamor of the city God speaks to me in His judgments, and all these things are seeds sent to me from His will.
>
> If these seeds would take root in my liberty, and if His will would grow from my freedom, I would become the love that He is, and my harvest would be His glory and my own joy.[6]

Bonaventure claimed that humanity was created poor insofar as every creature depends essentially and totally on the Creator. Each creature is a gift of God with an intrinsic value that is unique to itself. We know ourselves in our total dependency on God. Our existential poverty is what binds us to God and opens us up to God who is the origin of every good gift. The human person who is in relationship to God does not possess, but only receives. Our poverty is our receptivity; God fills the emptiness, so to speak.

When we truly ask, "Who am I?" we begin a life of poverty. This is the first question we must ask to come to know God. Bonaventure wrote that "No one comes to a full notion (notitiam) of God except through a true and proper notion of himself. No one rightly knows himself unless he recognizes his own nothingness."[7] We must recognize that we are not God but created by God out of nothing. Poverty is rooted in our creaturehood in that we are not equal to God. It means radical dependency since we come from another and are dependent on another for the very existence of life.

All of creation is contingent or essentially related, not just the human person. "The human person has no more claim to intrinsic being than a plant or animal, a star or a stone," the Himes brothers write.[8] This, of course, is not to deny the unique role the human person plays in the divine economy. We might say the "human person is the point in creation to which the fullness of the self-gift of God can be given. But the human person has been *created* as such."[9] Humans do not have a solo part in the creation story; rather, they are part of the cosmic chorus in praise of God. In this respect, all of creation is a grace-filled reality of God. It is a sacrament of God's abundant, self-diffusive goodness freely shared. The doctrine of creation out of nothing (*creatio ex nihilo*) is not a claim about how the universe came into being, but why it came into being at all. It discloses the fundamental poverty of the universe. "The universe has no intrinsic ground for existence."[10] It is a free gift of God's overflowing love. The great spiritual writers knew this simple truth. Augustine, for example, wrote in his *Confessions*:

> I asked the earth, and it said, "I am not he!" And all things in it con-
> fessed the same. I asked the sea and the deeps, and among living ani-
> mals the things that creep, and they answered, "We are not your

God! Seek you higher than us!" I asked the winds that blow: and all the air, with the dwellers therein, said, "Anaximenes was wrong. I am not God!" I asked the heavens, the sun, the moon, and the stars: "We are not the God whom you seek," said they....

"We are not God!" and again, "He made us!"[11]

Francis of Assisi also had a profound sense of God's goodness as the source of beauty and goodness in creation. In his *Major Legend of Saint Francis* Bonaventure wrote that "he would call creatures, no matter how small, by the name of 'brother' or 'sister' because he knew they shared with him the same beginning."[12] Rather than viewing the world from the top rung of the ladder of creation, Francis saw himself as part of creation. Poverty enabled him to realize his solidarity with creation. Instead of using creatures to ascend to God, he found God in all creatures and identified with them as brother and sister because he saw that they had the same primordial goodness as himself. By the end of his life Francis considered himself as a brother to all creation. All creation was his family. This was not some type of romantic love but a real insight: He found himself truly related to the stars, moon, sun, wind and earth. Everything spoke to him of God and he found God in and through created things. What allowed Francis entry into this experience of fraternity of all creation was poverty. Leonardo Boff explains that such poverty "is a way of being by which the individual lets things be what they are; one refuses to dominate them, subjugate them, and make them the objects of the will to power."[13] Required for such an embrace of poverty is a renunciation of the instinct to power, to the dominion over things. It is the desire for possession that stands between true communication between persons with each other and with all creation. As Francis became poor he became open to fraternity. Poverty was the way into the experience of universal brotherhood. Through poverty Francis recognized his own creatureliness, one creature among many creatures; one poor person amidst the diverse poverty of creation. He realized that, as a creature, he was "not over things, but together with them, like brothers and sisters of the same family."[14]

The poverty of creation reflects a God of gracious and generous love. Indeed, the only reason for anything to exist, according to Bonaventure, is the free gift of God's overflowing love. The universe comes into being because God loves it and wills to give God's self to it. As the Himes brothers state:

> Utterly dependent, creation is divinely gifted. Thus, to see creation as a whole or any creature in particular as what it is, namely, totally dependent on the gracious will of God, is to see revealed the grace which is its foundation in being. Since everything that is exists because of the free act of God—the overflowing *agape* that is the source of all being—then everything is a sacrament of the goodness and creative power of God.[15]

The poverty of created existence reveals the richness of divine presence, and in the poverty of creation, the human person is the fullest revelation of God. Poverty means receptivity, and creation is intended to be the womb of God's grace. Bonaventure indicated that the human person is "the poor one in the desert" simply because she or he is created. Although humans originally stood upright in creation, meaning that they had their heads pointed in the right direction, so to speak— toward God—they were originally poor, for they had been created out of nothing by another. As long as humans recognized and accepted their own poverty, they knew God. But when humans refused to be poor, they desired to possess rather than receive. This is the root of sin, Bonaventure claims, because humans chose to love their own good rather than receive the goods of the divine Giver. Bonaventure goes on to say that when we accept poverty as creatures we possess all because we possess God. Once we refuse that poverty in the desire to possess things we end up with nothing. In our refusal to accept the poverty of our humanity, we may end up destroying ourselves.

Francis of Assisi had a profound understanding of poverty as it relates to the human condition. His understanding of poverty goes hand in hand with his understanding of sin. In his second admonition he spoke of sin as self-appropriation. Just as when we eat we consume or take in things for ourselves, so, too, sin entered into the human condition when we started consuming for ourselves, symbolized by eating from the forbidden tree that we read about in the book of Genesis. Francis described sin as one of appropriating the gift of liberty and exalting ourselves over the goodness that surrounds us. To take what does not belong to us, to claim it as our own, and to use it for personal advancement is sin. Francis therefore would describe sin as: grasping, appropriating or grabbing, self-exalting and self-aggrandizing. The question is: What belongs to us? Does not my house, my car, my computer, my clothes and whatever else I own belong to me? Well, yes and no. If we purchased these goods legally we do own these goods. But how do we relate to them? Do we use them to fulfill our needs? Or do we possess them in such a way that we are unwilling to share them with others? Ownership may be a legal right but possessiveness is a value, an attitude.

There is a story of an old man who lived on a beautiful Greek island. When the time of his death approached he grasped a piece of the earth from his beloved homeland and clutched it in his hand. When he died and went to God, God asked him to let go of the earth in his hand so that he could enter into heaven. He refused. Thus the gates of heaven would not open for him. Soon after his wife died and went to heaven, as did his sons and relatives. Each time a family member entered into heaven, God asked the man to let go so as to join his loved ones in glory. Each time he refused to let go. Finally after many generations had passed and those born after him went before him into the glory of heaven, God asked the man to let go. Finally the man conceded and opened his hand. When he did so he was shocked to discover that there was nothing in his hand. The earth he had clung to was not there; indeed, it was never there to begin with because it was not his, but a gift of God.[16]

This story is a good example of what Francis and Clare maintain, namely that we possess nothing except our own vices and sins. Only when we live as poor persons do we recognize that the goods of this world do not belong to us and, thus, we may not possess them. Rather, they are gifts from God. Oftentimes we are too self-absorbed to see God's goodness at the center of our lives and at the center of our world. We call this type of self-absorption sin.

Sin, in Bonaventure's thought, is a turning away from God and a turning toward self in such a way that we become bent over, blinded in intellect, and entangled in an infinite number of questions. We wander about in the world looking for goodness (or love) because we are unable to recognize it within ourselves. Blinded in intellect and distorted in our desires, we start grabbing for ourselves what does not truly belong to us. Instead of being poor persons radically dependent on God, we make ourselves little gods and centers of our universe. We use everything for our own purposes and we take from others what does not rightly belong to us. When we strip the world of the common good that is God's gift to creation, we create a new system of poverty. We move from the true poverty of radical dependence to the false poverty of greed. We think we never have enough and thus we set out to acquire more and more things at the expense of other people and creation itself. The sin of refusing our poverty is injustice. Our need to accumulate and possess everything we can cling to separates us from other people and the natural world, and we lord it over others through domination and power. We lose our sense of piety or true relatedness. The world becomes not only stripped of its goodness but relationships are broken because we fail to recognize our dependence on one another, and thus we fail to acknowledge our dependence on God.

Bonaventure says that the sin of humans is really sin against the Son of God. The human desire for power is sin against the One who is the perfect image of God and thus equal to God. The Son of God, he says, accepts the poverty of human condition to show that equality with God is not something to grasp. On the cross, God himself becomes poor. The poverty of the cross, Bonaventure indicates, is a mystery of poverty because on the cross God is not "possessing" but fully "communicating" the mystery of his love in his radical openness to and acceptance of the human person. In the crucified Christ strength is expressed in weakness and the powerful God becomes the poor man.

Poverty is manifest in the historical career of Jesus and expressed in the naked figure on the cross who invites us to follow him, placing our absolute trust in God alone. The mystery of poverty is the recreation of the human person where one can stand before God without demands. Poverty returns one to the center of original innocence because it is fulfillment of new law which does not promise temporal goods but love.[17]

We might think that Francis arrived at a deep understanding of poverty through renunciation of his material possessions. But this is not entirely true. Nowhere did he write of living *sine rebus huius mundi* (without the things of this world) or in destitution. Usually he wrote of living *sine proprio*, that is, without anything of one's own. The central question of poverty was, for Francis, what can I really call my own? Although material poverty was important to him, it was not the goal. Rather material poverty was an outward sign of a much deeper, interior poverty. We might say that material poverty is sacramental in nature. It points to an interior poverty of spirit that Jesus proclaimed in the beatitudes: "Blessed are the poor in spirit, for theirs is the kingdom of heaven" (Matthew 5:3). Thus, material poverty is the first step (but a necessary one) toward true poverty in which we recognize that everything we have, including our lives, is gift. Without material poverty, true poverty is difficult to nurture. But without true poverty, material poverty is absurd. In the quest for wholeness, poverty must be sacramental in nature, a continuous striving to live more deeply in the spirit of nonpossessiveness.

Francis was a keen observer of the human condition and his understanding of poverty as the core of humanity came from the most basic lesson of life—living with others. Although Francis rarely spoke of poverty in his writings (which is surprising since others made poverty the characteristic mark of his life), he did highlight three areas in which poverty is placed in an everyday context as we seek right relationship with God. These areas are: (1) our inner selves, (2) our relations with others, and (3) our relations with God.[18] With regard to the inner self, Francis saw how human persons can cling to the gifts that God has given them for example, skills, wisdom, knowledge, ability with language, good looks and riches. In "Admonition VII" he says, "Those people are put to death by the letter who only wish to know the words alone, that they might be esteemed wiser than others."[18] It is not unusual to encounter those who want to "show off" their knowledge or win an argument or have the last word or the most intelligent word. Humans tend to cling to knowledge as a possession that distinguishes them over and above others. Such people, according to Francis, are not poor. Similarly, those who are preoccupied with themselves, whether with regard to health, family, work, honor or reputation, are not poor. Did you ever meet someone where the entire conversation is focused on his or her job, family or health? Where self-preoccupation so predominates the conversation that it would not matter if you were an earthworm or a tadpole or whether or not you were listening? Such a person is not poor.

It is not only in relation to ourselves, however, that we cling to things. Francis indicated that we tend to cling to attitudes and behaviors in relation to others. I have known people who can recall past incidences with intense emotion and detail, even though the person who sparked their emotional outrage has long been dead. People can cling to the ghosts of the past and refuse to live in the present. Such are not poor persons and they usually fail to enjoy the presence of God's love. Francis considered anger, or being disturbed at the sin of another, as the mark of possessiveness. He suggested that we should turn our attention to the sinner rather than the sin. Otherwise we cling to our anger and become upset because we self-righteously judge the one who sins.[19] Anger can dissipate prayer and prevent us from being opened up to God. In "Admonition XIV," for example, Francis writes:

> There are many who, while insisting on prayers and obligations, inflict many abstinences and punishments upon their bodies. But they are immediately offended and disturbed about a single word which seems to be harmful to their bodies or about something which might be taken away from them. These people are not poor in spirit.[20]

Francis' words remind us of Paul's advice to the Corinthians: "If I give away all my possessions, and if I hand over my body so that I may boast, but do not have love, I gain nothing" (1 Corinthians 13:3). Francis, like Paul, reminds us that without love material poverty is worthless and perhaps sinful. We are called to "let go and let God"—to let go of everything we cling to and allow God to be the center of our lives; not to possess anything (or anyone) for ourselves but, as Clare indicates, to possess God alone.

Of course the primary center of possession in the human person is the will. This is our most valuable center because it is the very core of our attachments. The human will is the source of free choice, the decision-making center of the human person. It is most vulnerable because it can be easily threatened. We cling to our will when we are challenged or threatened in our personhood. When it comes to the will, we even like to barter with God. We say things like, "I will go to church again if God makes me rich." The will, in Francis' view, is the place of freedom, and because it is the place of freedom, it is the root of sin because here we decide if we will grab and appropriate for ourselves or share with others.

Francis perceived that the will's self-centeredness can be transformed only by being other-centered. The virtue of obedience can be a means of transformation because obedience requires a listening to another and letting go of our wills out of love for one another. Obedience does not necessarily entail having a superior, commanding officer or a demanding parent. Rather, obedience can take place between friends, lovers, family or in community. Obedience does not mean a hierarchy of order, a top-down chain of command, but a relationship of mutuality whereby the power of love is greater than the power of self-will. Rooted in the power of love, obedience becomes an expression of the embrace of poverty, letting go of what we have made our own, our wills, and entrusting ourselves into the hands of another. Obedience does not demand so much to do the will of another but rather to give oneself to the other out of love. To be obedient therefore means truly listening to the other, respecting and desiring the best for the other. Jesus was the model of true obedience, according to Francis, because he desired nothing other than to do the will of the Father, that is, to love the Father unto death. Obedience, therefore, can restore our fallen self-will and direct us to the will of God which is God's love for us, even as that love comes to us through our relationship with one another. Without obedience we become isolated and privatized individuals, locked up and enclosed within ourselves and cut off from the lifeline of God's love in the ordinary human person—our neighbor, sister, brother, husband, child—and the simple ordinary goodness of everyday creation.

Obedience, as the fruit of poverty, manifests itself in the right relationships of community. Francis saw poverty as the basis of community because poverty is the basis of interdependence. When we are in need, we are dependent on others. He saw Christ as the model and center of community because just as Jesus lived on alms and was poor, so too, our poverty means to be dependent on others (and thus on God). In short, ownership can make community impossible because when we own things in a spirit of possession, we do not need others. Ownership as possessiveness can create self-sufficiency, independence and therefore divisiveness. The spirit of possessiveness can place us over and against others. Francis indicated that neither work nor shared vision brings people together but the Spirit of love. Poverty as radical dependence is the language of love, a concern for one another. It is the language that says, "I need you, your gifts, your goodness, your ideas and your help. Who and what you are is essential to me because without you I really cannot be me." Poverty is the great leveler because it makes everyone dependent on and open to one another. It is a type of obedience because it involves a letting go of our wills out of love for one another. Poverty speaks the language of love for one another because it ultimately says, "I need you to help complete my life." Unless we are willing to let go of what we cling to in relation to one another, we fail in poverty and thus we fail to appreciate the gifts of God's love planted in each unique human being and, we might say, in every aspect of creation. Only a life that does not possess or cling to things is free and open to receive the love of God in the humble goodness of creation.

Poverty reminds us of the deepest truth of our human existence; that we are created by God and are dependent on God in an absolute sense. It is the sister of humility since it prompts us to recognize that *all we have is gift*. Humility is the acceptance of being what we are, with our strengths and weaknesses, and responding in love to the gift of being. Humility can open one to the renewing spirit of grace and make possible the return of creation to the Father. Thomas Merton said that if we were truly humble we would not bother about ourselves at all, only with God.[21] Such an idea seems possible only for the saints. Yet when we are free from attachments, from clinging to things, then we are able to pursue our spiritual goals, to really live in love and devote ourselves to a life of adoration. This does not mean turning our attention away from earth to an imaginable place called heaven. Rather, to adore God is to see the goodness of every created thing on this marvelous planet Earth circling in a galaxy of stars. It is to realize that everything is created by God, reflects the power, wisdom and goodness of God, and is destined to share life in God. Poverty allows us to contemplate the goodness of God in creation because it makes us free to see things for what they are, unrepeatable, unclonable, loved-into-being gifts of God. Only one who can taste the world and see it as an expression of God's love can renounce the spirit of possessing it. In human relationships, poverty allows us to be open to one another, to receive and share with one another. Poverty is the basis of personhood because it involves *kenosis* or self-emptying. Just as the persons of the Trinity are distinguished by their sharing of love, so too, poverty is the basis of true human community. Only care for one another truly humanizes life. Barbara Fiand claims that the blessedness of the poor (the economically poor), that which has them stand in solidarity, is their need and their knowledge of their need. It is this need that renders them open, receptive, grateful.[22] Those who are open enough and empty enough, in need enough to receive and to give forth what they have received through gratitude are poor persons who can teach us the way of poverty as our pathway into God.

Clare of Assisi did not elaborate on the poverty of the human person but she knew it in the depths of her soul. She fought for the "privilege of poverty" because she knew that if she failed to be dependent on others, she would ultimately fail to be dependent on God. Like Francis, she firmly believed in a God enfleshed in fragile human nature—Incarnation. Had she sought a nice, clean, fresh, minty type of God in heaven, she might have opted for more autonomy. But she believed that God has come among us and revealed to us, in the poverty of being human, how to live united in love, to God and to another. She realized that only the poor and humble can share in the poor and humble love of God. Clare's path to God through the depths of poverty impels us to admit that real relationship with God requires true humble humanity. Only when we come to the truth of who we are (and who we are not) as poor persons can we come to that place of vulnerability in our lives where God can enter in. Only then can we know what it means to be a human person embedded in a world of goodness.

QUESTIONS FOR REFLECTION

1. Do you live as a poor person? If not, what prevents you from embracing your poverty?

2. How do you understand the relation between material poverty and spiritual poverty?

3. Does poverty help you become more dependent on others? Do you see yourself in need of others or do you prefer autonomy and individualism?

4. What helps and hinders your openness to God and others?

NOTES

[1] Clare of Assisi, "The First Letter to Agnes of Prague," 6 (*Écrits*, 84), *Early Documents*, p. 35.

[2] Ramon Llull, *The Book of the Lover and the Beloved*, 97. Mark D. Johnston, trans. (Warminster: Aris and Phillips, 1995), p. 39.

[3] Francis of Assisi, "The Earlier Rule," 9.2–4, *FA:ED* 1, p. 70.

[4] This quote from the Letter to the Corinthians was a favorite of Bonaventure and he referred to it frequently in his Commentary on Luke's Gospel. See

Bonaventure "Commentary on Gospel of Luke: Chapters 1–8," 2:7, Volume VIII, Part I, *Works of St. Bonaventure*, Robert J. Karris, ed. (New York: Franciscan Institute, 2001), p. 150.

[5] Kenneth and Michael Himes, "The Sacrament of Creation: Toward an Environmental Theology," *Commonweal* (January 26, 1990), p. 45.

[6] Thomas Merton, *New Seeds of Contemplation* (New York: New Directions, 1961), pp. 16–17.

[7] Bonaventure, *Perfectione evangelium* q. 1, concl. (V, 120-121), quoted in Wayne Hellmann, "Poverty: The Franciscan Way to God," *Theology Digest* 22 (1974), p. 339.

[8] Himes, "Sacrament of Creation," p. 45.

[9] Himes, "Sacrament of Creation," p. 45.

[10] Himes, "Sacrament of Creation," p. 45.

[11] Augustine, *The Confessions of Saint Augustine*, John K. Ryan, trans. (New York: Image, 1960), p. 234.

[12] Bonaventure, "The Major Legend of Saint Francis" 8.6 in *FA:ED II*, p. 590.

[13] Quoted in Kenneth and Michael Himes, "Creation and an Environmental Ethic," in *Fullness of Faith: The Public Significance of Theology* (Mahwah, N.J.: Paulist, 1993), p. 119.

[14] Himes, *Fullness of Faith*, p. 119.

[15] Himes, "The Sacrament of Creation," p. 45.

[16] A slightly different version of this story is told by Ronald Rolheiser in his book *The Shattered Lantern* (New York: Crossroad, 2001), pp. 187–188. While Rolheiser says that he heard the story from John Shea, he attributes its source to a remythologization of Nikos Kazantakis's own life in his *Report to Greco* (New York: Simon and Schuster, 1960). See *The Shattered Lantern*, p. 205, n7.

[17] Hellman, p. 343.

[18] The basis of this section is Regis Armstrong's discussion on poverty in *Francis of Assisi: Writings for a Gospel Life* (New York: Crossroad, 1994), pp. 152–165. See especially p. 154.

[19] Francis of Assisi, "Admonition VII" in *FA:ED I*, p. 132.

[20] In his *Earlier Rule*, Francis writes, "Let all the brothers be careful not to slander or engage in disputes...let them not quarrel among themselves...let them love one another...let them not grumble...let them not consider the least sins of others." See *Earlier Rule*, 11 in *FA:ED I*, p.72. See also Admonitions VIII, XIV. In Admonition VIII Francis says, "[W]hoever envies his brother the good that the Lord says or does in him incurs a sin of blasphemy because he envies the Most High Himself Who says and does every good thing (*FA:ED I*, p. 132).

[21] Francis of Assisi, "Admonition XIV," in *FA:ED I*, p. 133.

[22] Thomas Merton, *New Seeds of Contemplation*, p. 189.

[23] Barbara Fiand, *Living the Vision: Religious Vows in an Age of Change* (New York: Crossroad, 1990), p. 59.

Chapter Three

THE MIRROR OF THE CROSS

Poverty as the path to life is difficult for us to grasp but the type of poverty that Clare cherished was not material want or need itself, but that poverty which spoke to her of the love of God. Clare saw this poverty in the figure of the crucified Christ on the cross. Since she lived an enclosed and restricted life, it is likely that the icon of the crucified and glorified Christ at San Damiano was one of the few images she saw throughout her sixty years of earthly life. It was an image she knew well and pondered deeply within her. Her writings indicate that the cross was not a static event for Clare; rather, it was a living and dynamic experience of God. In her third and fourth letters to Agnes, she describes the cross as a mirror. The title "mirror mystic" is an appropriate one for Clare because it describes not only her deep love of Christ and desire to follow him, but also of what she considered essential to Christian identity, to become a mirror image of Christ.[1]

In the Middle Ages the mirror was just coming into vogue both as an object of beauty and a symbol of the spiritual life. Regis Armstrong indicates that

> Two styles of mirror emerge in the literature of the Middle Ages: the instructive, and the exemplary...."[I]nstructive" spiritual literature... assists us to know an ideal and to confront ourselves in the light of it.... [W]orks in the "exemplary" spiritual literature...[present] a normative knowledge or a vision of self leading to moral or spiritual purification.[2]

Many spiritual writers, for example, used the symbol of the mirror to describe the soul as a mirror of God. The theme of the mirror can be found in the letters of Saint Paul. In his letters to the Corinthians, for example, Paul writes: "For now we see in a mirror, dimly, but then we will see face to face" (1 Corinthians 13:12a) and, "And all of us, with unveiled faces, seeing the glory of the Lord as though reflected in a mirror, are being transformed into the same image from one degree of glory to another; for this comes from the Lord, the Spirit" (2 Corinthians 3:18). Just as a mirror, empty in itself, reflects back what is given to it, so, too, the soul purified and illumined reflects the presence of God. It was not unusual to find the mirror symbol in the spiritual writings of women, especially the German mystics and Beguine women.[3] However, Clare of Assisi used the concept of the mirror in a particular way, not to describe the soul as symbol of God but the human person as image of God. Clare saw Christ crucified as the true image of God and the image in which we are created. Clare indicated that Christ is the image in whom Agnes would find the true meaning of her life in God.

What does it mean to say that Christ is the image in which we are created? And how do we relate to Christ as the "mirror image" of our lives? Before we say what the image is, perhaps we can indicate what it is not. It is not being God by having control and domination over other people or the earth itself. It is not a matter of wielding power and authority or manipulating others to one's advantage. To be an image of God is to be relational, to love, to suffer with another and ultimately to lay down one's life for a friend. In the first chapter of Genesis we read that God created humans in his image:

> So God created humankind in his image,
>   in the image of God he created them;
>   male and female he created them. (Genesis 1:27)

The author of Genesis indicates that God not only creates humans but he creates them male and female. Why did not God create a single-gendered species in his image? It is not that God is gendered or bisexual; rather, the story of Genesis indicates that God is relational. To be the image of God, the human being must be relational.[4] Relationship is what defines the human person in his or her divine dignity.

While the Old Testament tells us that we are created in the image of God, still the idea of being an image of God is vague, especially if we look around the world today. What does the image of God look like amidst war, violence and ruin? Bonaventure's theology is helpful here because he emphasizes the Word of God as true image. In his commentary on the *Sentences* he distinguishes between the Son of God as image and the human person as image. The Son, he states, is the image of the Father since it is from the Father that the Son proceeds by nature of the Father's goodness. Because the Son is *from* the Father (*a quo*), the Son is the perfect image and expression of the Father, sharing the same nature and, thus, expressing the Father totally and completely. As he states in the *Hexaëmeron:* "For from all eternity the Father begets a Son similar to Himself and expresses Himself and a likeness similar to Himself, and in so doing He expresses the sum total of His [active] potency."[5] The Word is the Father's total and perfect self-expression as supreme loving Being and source of all that is or can be. While the second person is the immanent Image of the Father, there is an image of God in the world of creation and that is the human person. Inasmuch as the human is oriented toward the proper image that is in God, she or he is tending toward the image, whereas the Son, in his whole being, *is* the image of the Father. Bonaventure sees the congruent relationship between God and humanity specifically in the relationship between the Word and humanity. The human person is an image of God not in the general sense of being "like" God but in the specific sense of being "like" the Son. That is why Jesus Christ, the incarnate Word of God, shows us what it means to be an image of God in our humanity. The human person is created as an image of the Image of God and that Image is Jesus Christ.

The idea that humans are formed "to the image" rather than "as image" is important to understand Clare's theology of image. The term "to the image" underscores the congruent relationship between humanity and the Word, which Clare perceives in her own way. To say that human persons are created "to the image" (*ad imaginem*) connotes both a structure and a goal, since the Word is the true and perfect image in which humans are created. For Bonaventure the Incarnation becomes the point of departure for understanding the deepest truth about the human person and his or her relation to the divine. Bonaventure's theology of the image impels us to admit that we are "Word people" called to incarnate the Word in our own time and place.

While every person has the capacity to be an image of God, there are few who live this image fully, perhaps because we have no clear idea of what it means to be image of God. But Clare saw this image visibly expressed in the crucified Christ. She described the crucified Christ as a mirror because in gazing upon this mirror we see a true reflection of ourselves—our image. Christ reflects back to us what we are to be in our lives. The notion of the mirror to describe who we are in relation to God is a profound one because mirrors are such an integral part of our everyday lives. The mirror reveals to us how we look. Do we look young and beautiful or old and weary? Do we look too fat? Too thin? Too tall? Too short? The mirror tells us how we will appear before others and whether or not others will find us attractive, repulsive or ordinary. Without mirrors we simply do not know how we appear. Many people carry small mirrors around with them so that they may periodically check their looks. When vanity predominates, the rear-view mirror of the car becomes a fixture in a mobile beauty salon.

Whereas the mirrors we peer into in our everyday world give us a glimpse of ourselves, we see only the exterior image and not the full image of who we are; the image we see is incomplete. What if we had mirrors that allowed us to look within ourselves as well? What if we peered into a mirror that reflected our hearts, minds or souls? What would we see and would we like what we see? Clare asks Agnes of Prague to gaze into the mirror of the crucified Christ so as to discover who she is inwardly and what she reflects outwardly. Only in the mirror of the cross, Clare indicates, do we truly see who we are and what we are called to be by becoming transformed into the image of Christ. Agnes is to look into the mirror of the cross to see her image, which Clare identifies as the mind, soul and heart. She writes:

Place your mind before the mirror of eternity!
Place your soul *in the brilliance of glory*!
Place your heart in the *figure of the* divine *substance*!
And *transform* your entire being *into the image*
of the Godhead Itself through contemplation.[6]

Clare's words remind us of Jesus' command: "You shall love the Lord your God with all your heart, and with all your soul, and with all your strength, and with all your mind; and your neighbor as yourself" (Luke 10:27). What Clare indicates is that to love God with your whole mind, soul and heart is to contemplate God, and contemplation cannot take place apart from transformation: Thus, Agnes is to place her mind, soul and heart in the "mirror of eternity." I wonder how many of us look on the cross as the "mirror of eternity"—a reflection of eternity in the crucified Christ. We rarely think of eternity hanging on a cross unless of course we understand that eternity is God, God is love and God's love is expressed in the crucified Christ. For that is what Clare says: The mirror of eternity is the crucified Christ. God is revealed as all-embracing, outpouring love in the figure of the crucified Christ who is the splendor of eternal glory, the brilliance of eternal light and the mirror without blemish. In the cross, we see a reflection of the eternal God who is the fullness of love.

In her fourth letter to Agnes, Clare says that she is to gaze upon the mirror each day. What does it mean to gaze daily upon the mirror of the cross? There are stargazers, baby-gazers, lover-gazers but who gazes on the crucified Christ? To gaze is not simply to see. Rather to gaze is to be drawn into the object which one sees. We may liken a gaze to a visual experience of embrace. Miroslav Volf describes a "phenomenology of embrace" that may help us understand the power of gazing. An embrace, Volf writes, begins with opening the arms.

> Open arms are a gesture of the body reaching for the other. They are a sign of discontent with my own self-enclosed identity, a code of *desire* for the other. I do not want to be myself only; I want the other to be part of who I am and I want to be part of the other.[7]

A self that is "full of itself" can neither receive the other nor make genuine movement toward the other.[8] Open arms signify that I have created space in myself for the other to come in and that I have made a movement out of myself so as to enter the space created by the other.[9] One does not stop at the embrace, though, for the embrace is not meant to make two bodies one, to dissolve one body into the other. The arms must open again; this preserves the genuine identity of each subject of the embrace.[10] Nor should we try to understand the other if we are to preserve the genuine identity of the other in the embrace. If we try to understand the other on our own terms, we make the other into a projection of ourselves or try to absorb the other into ourselves. A genuine embrace entails the ability not to understand but to accept the other as a question right in the midst of the embrace, and to let go, allowing the question of the other to remain mystery.[11]

The gaze on the crucified Christ is an embrace of the heart, a desire to allow the otherness of God's love into our lives. Therefore it can never be an immediate vision; rather, it is a daily encounter with a God of humble love who is hidden in fragile humanity. Gazing is not simply physical sight like other physical senses that help situate us in an environment. Rather, gazing is of the heart, by which the heart "opens its arms," so to speak, to allow the Spirit of God's love to enter. Gazing requires a space within the heart to receive what we see and to "embrace" what we see. Poverty helps create this space because when we are free of things that we possess or that possess us we are able to see more clearly and to receive what we see within us.

Gazing on the crucified Christ, as a way of encountering God, can be difficult because we are not attracted to crucified bodies or suffering humanity. We tend to deny suffering and shun the disfigured, the abandoned and the dying. We erase their presence by ignoring them, pretending they do not exist, so that we may direct our attention to beauty, wealth and health. Yet, according to Clare, God is revealed in fragile, frail and crucified flesh. In the scandalous figure of the Crucified we encounter the power of God's love. Clare directs us to taste this God of hidden sweetness in the crucified body of Jesus bound to the cross.

Because gazing is a penetrating encounter with the other, it is also an experience of tasting the other, of taking the other into oneself—experiencing, but not annihilating the other. To gaze, therefore, requires openness to grace. It is to be open to the Spirit of the Lord, for it is the Spirit within us who really gazes or, we might say, who "embraces" the God of humble love.[12] The Spirit who dwells in the depths of the human heart searches the depths of God in the crucified flesh of Jesus and cries out "Abba!" It is the Spirit who joins us to Christ and leads us into the embrace of the humble love of God.

The importance of gazing into the mirror of the cross cannot be over-emphasized. For we live in an age where crucifying others has become sport in the same way that the torture of early Christian martyrs provided entertainment for the Romans. In a recent article on torture, the author noted how a young, twenty-two-year-old Afghani taxi driver was wrongfully accused and imprisoned. While in prison he was chained to the ceiling of his cell, suspended there for three days. His legs were beaten to a pulp and his arms became dislocated from their sockets. According to the author, "they flapped like a bird's broken wings when he was taken down for interrogation, as Jesus' arms may have done had he been taken down from the cross before three hours."[13] During the whole time of his torture, he continuously cried out to Allah for mercy but, like Jesus, felt abandoned in the darkness of his suffering. The soldiers who tortured him apparently laughed every time he cried out to Allah and taunted him even more to the point where, after enduring broken limbs and serious burns, he gave up his spirit. He left behind a wife and a small child who were probably waiting for him to return home after that fatal night of picking up the wrong person just to make a decent wage as a taxi driver.

While such a story is meant to awaken us to the cruel streak imbedded in humanity, it also awakens us to the violence of the human heart that knows no limit in the absence of God. Clare's gaze into the mirror of the cross is not only a means of personal transformation but a means of restoring justice and dignity to the human person by allowing God's presence to show itself in one other than ourselves. Because we find it

difficult to accept the other as one who is different from us without pro-
jecting ourselves onto the other, gazing into the mirror of the cross
requires the vision of a poor person. The person who knows that she or
he is radically dependent on God must make space within the heart to
let God in. The poor person is one who is open and free to gaze with
the eyes of the heart, the eyes of penetrating vision that can touch,
taste and experience the image of God on the cross. Clare invites Agnes
to look at Christ's bruised and violated beauty, to embrace him, touch
him, perceive his fragrance, hear his voice, and taste the hidden sweetness which only his friends experience. This gaze is a type of "reading"
insofar as we are confronted by the Word of God in our flesh. We are
to study this Word with a penetrating gaze and become inwardly familiar with the image in which we are created.

For Clare the use of the mirror as a tool for the spiritual life is not
unlike the use of Scripture in the monastic tradition. It helps her to
reflect, ponder and consider her life more deeply as a follower and imitator of Christ. Just as in the monastic tradition, in which one prayerfully reads Scripture, slowly ruminating on the Word of God (lectio div-
ina), Clare asks Agnes to "read" the Word made flesh by gazing on the
mirror of the cross. Agnes is to "read" with the eye of the heart, penetrating the depths of the image she beholds, as one who is in search of
fine pearls. This type of penetrating gaze, Clare says, is the path to contemplation. Contemplation begins not by penetrating ourselves to discover our own faults and failings but by going out of ourselves to see
the sufferings of the other, by gazing on the other. No one can contemplate God, in Clare's view, unless one learns to gaze. In a similar vein,
Bonaventure wrote, "Christ goes away when the mind attempts to
behold this wisdom through intellectual eyes; since it is not the intellect that can go in there, but the heart."[14] For the Franciscans, God is
love and only one who lives in love can *see* and thus contemplate God.

Gazing on the mirror of the cross each day is not only an outward
movement for Clare but a self-reflective one as well. For the mirror of
the cross is not only the image of God but the image of our humanity
as well. If we are unsure what it means to be the image of God, Clare

reminds us that we are confronted by this image in the outstretched figure of Christ nailed to a cross. The image of our humanity is shown to us in the disturbing reality of the Crucified.

Clare recognizes that the human person is a limited creature who, being created and contingent, is subject to all the difficulties of limitations, including the fragmentation of sin. However, humans also have the capacity to transcend themselves, to go beyond self out of concern or love for another. When we come to authentic personhood in the mirror of the cross, our image, we are on the path to contemplation and transformation in God. Clare helps Agnes to contemplate her own image by studying the figure of the Crucified. She writes:

> Look at the border of this mirror, that is, the poverty of Him who was placed in a manger and wrapped in swaddling clothes.
> O marvelous humility!
> O astonishing poverty!
> The King of angels,
> the Lord of heaven and earth,
> is laid in a manger!
> Then, at the surface of the mirror, consider the holy humility, the blessed poverty, the untold labors and burdens that He endured for the redemption of the whole human race. Then, in the depth of this same mirror, contemplate the ineffable charity that led Him to suffer on the wood of the Cross and to die there the most shameful kind of death.[15]

The San Damiano cross that Clare gazed upon does not depict a lonely, abandoned figure of Christ but a crucified-glorified Christ surrounded by a community of disciples. Michael Guinan has suggested that the San Damiano cross is a visual representation of the Gospel of John which includes the image of Jesus as priest. We know from Francis' own writings that Jesus' "high-priestly prayer" at the Last Supper, where he prays that all may be one (John 17), was especially important to him.[16] In Jesus, the glory of God is revealed, and the offering of his life is to the glory of the Father. Christ is the center of unity between God and creation since he is the Word through whom God is made known and the One in whom all are gathered into the unity of God's love. While Clare saw the mystery of God as love in the cross, she also saw the mystery of the human person marked by the poverty, humility, and charity of the crucified Christ. Clare called the marks of poverty, humility and charity "footprints" because they help us identify the presence of Christ not only outside ourselves but within ourselves as well. They are the footprints of the image of God in which we are created. Whatever we say about Jesus in this mirror, we are saying about ourselves as well.

The humanity of Jesus is our humanity, and because our humanity is the place where God comes to meet us, the cross shows us the truth about ourselves. Clare's spirituality is profound. For as mirror and image, the life of the crucified Christ is our life, his poverty is our poverty, his humility is our humility, his capacity to love is our capacity to love. Clare says to Agnes, "gaze upon that mirror each day."[17] By this she means look deeply at who you are in the mirror of the cross. When we gaze into the mirror of the cross, what do we see? Do we see our poverty, our poverty of being, our existence which comes from God and is dependent on God? Do we recognize our dependence on God not simply because God is "bigger and better" but because we are finite, created beings? Do we see God as the power of love to raise to life what might be dead for us? Do we accept ourselves as good and lovable, as the unique, created beings God intended in Christ from all eternity? Do we see God's dependence on us to make Christ a visible, living presence in the world? If we can begin to look at the borders and surfaces of our lives and see there more than mere existence or sameness, if we can begin to see that each border and surface is replete with meaning, then we can begin to look below the surface, into the heart of our image which reflects the heart of God who is deeply in love with creation.

Are we scandalously in love with creation as well? Clare's theology of the mirror is not simply a means of self-discovery but, even more so, it is the visible expression of what we are created for, the meaning and purpose of our lives, as they are reflected to us in the figure of the crucified Christ. Her thought finds a note of comparison to the German mystic Meister Eckhart, for whom God's sending is symbolized by a mirror image. Just as a mirror is empty in itself and receives its being by mirroring, so too, without the countenance gazing into it, it is nothing. It is the gaze into the mirror that brings the mirror *as* mirror into being. At the same time, however, the mirror ceases to be noticed, since the person gazing into it is absorbed only in what she or he sees. Barbara Fiand explains Eckhart's thought by saying: "The being in the mirror, therefore, is the being of the mirrored. That which makes the mirror image what it is is the countenance reflected in the mirror, not the mirror image on its own."[18] This idea is very similar to what Clare perceives, namely, that the mirror image and the mirrored image are the same. As Fiand writes: "The mirror image gives itself to the one who looks at it and whom it mirrors. The mirror image does not only come from its 'other,' receiving its being from the 'other,' it also directs itself toward its 'other' and is what it is *for* its 'other.'"[19] The poverty of the mirror is such that without the "other" whom it mirrors, it would virtually cease to be a mirror. In the same way, the mirror of the cross is not an objective thing "out there" but rather finds its meaning only in view of those who gaze upon it and who, therefore, see themselves reflected in it.

Because the mirror of the cross mediates the opposites of emptiness and fullness, it is the place of contemplation for Clare. It is where we learn that contemplation is more than time alone with God or enlightened consciousness. Contemplation is to see with the eye of the heart, to feel with the heart, to perceive what analysis alone cannot explain. It is to see and recognize the charity hidden in suffering. Many people see but few understand the human person as the image of God. It takes a depth of self-reflection to see the love of God in one's own life in order to see the depth of God's love in the fragile and often suffering lives of others. Only those who have come to that place of poverty deep within can see into the depths of the heart of God, even as God is hidden in the ordinary flesh of another human person. Only those who can see into the depths of God can become truly images of God because they can see into the depths of themselves as well. As we see, so we love, and as we love, so we are transformed in love. The mirror of the cross tells us: *This is what you are: a humble bruised and broken person totally dependent on God. This is what you are called to be: a vessel of self-giving love.* The image we see in the mirror of the cross, the broken vessel of Christ's body as the outpouring gift of God's love, is what we are to be as image of God.

Although we find it difficult to see this image of God within ourselves, we may see this image of the crucified Christ in other people who, in pouring out their lives for others do, indeed, reflect God. The person who visits the sick in the hospital reveals the image of God. The person who gives up a seat on a crowded bus for another reveals the image of God. The soldier who puts his life on the line to save his comrades is the image of God, and the child who picks flowers for an elderly neighbor is the image of God. We see the mirror of the Crucified not on a wall but in living human persons. The person of the Crucified is reflected in our neighbors, our parents, our sisters and brothers and in persons we meet along the way. We know God, and we know ourselves in God, when we know one another and know ourselves in the other. The image of Christ that each of us is created to be is the way God's presence is renewed in the world. Each of us is meant to be a mirror reflecting the face of the eternal God.

But what exactly makes us an image of God? Is it something we are born with? Or do we grow into this image? Is it an inviolable core of the human person or a capacity that each human person has, that when acted upon becomes an imitation of God's love? Is it rooted simply in the fact that we are created, or is it that we are created as relational beings? In her own way Clare addresses these questions by pointing to the fact that to be the image of God is to be in relationship—not just any relationship—the relationship that will reflect the perfection of love. The deepest center of each person, the soul, must be informed (an act of the mind) by love. When we come to know ourselves, we come to know God, and when we come to know God, we enter the heart of enduring love.

Clare is aware of the immense potential of the human person as image of God, as she writes, "Indeed, it is now clear that the soul of a faithful person, the most worthy of all creatures because of the grace of God, is greater than heaven itself."[20] Yet she also knows the human person's ability to efface God by wrongful choices, as she continues in her letter to Agnes, ". . .since the heavens and the rest of creation cannot contain their Creator and only the faithful soul is His dwelling place and throne, and this only through the charity that the wicked lack."[21] On one hand Clare makes the astonishing claim that the human person can possess the Creator since "the faithful soul is His dwelling place and throne," and then she tells us how—through charity. It is love that makes us "possessors of God" or makes us like God, for God is love, and only love can possess love.

While everyone has the capacity for love, not everyone acts out of love. Obviously, for Clare, the wicked do not, as she writes: "How many... let themselves be deceived, for, even though their pride may reach the skies and their heads touch the clouds, in the end they are as forgotten as a dung-heap!"[22] And who are the wicked? Are we among them? Are the wicked those who do bad things or those who fail in love? We might say, for Clare, the wicked are those who fail in love, who are so preoccupied with themselves that they deceive themselves by looking into the wrong mirrors, mirrors that distort their image and make them think they are something other than what they really are. We wind up, in Clare's words, in a "dung-heap." We may attain material success but if we have failed to learn how to love we miss out on the heart of life.

To look into the mirror of the cross is to realize that we are called to be images of God, and to be images of God we are called into relationships of love. How do we come to that place in life where we can transcend our self-concerns and self-centeredness, where we reach out to others instead of reaching out for ourselves, where we are free to lay down our lives if necessary out of love for another? For Clare, we must gaze daily on the mirror of the cross. In this mirror is the reflection of humanity, what we are and what we are called to be. We may not see ourselves at first, for it may seem that the figure we behold in the mirror of the cross is totally different from us. But when we see with the heart, when we "gaze" into the mirror, then the figure we see is no different from the one who gazes. Clare calls us to a depth of self-reflection, and the crucified Christ is the image that helps us see who we are. If we can see the truth of ourselves through contemplation, our own poverty, humility and charity, then we can contemplate the presence of God in our neighbors, brothers and sisters and those in whom God is hidden. To contemplate God's love for us and the limitations of our humanity should purify us of false images and liberate us to love beyond measure.

For Clare, the poor, especially the spiritually poor, can gaze freely on a God of crucified love and see joy where others see sorrow. They can see the depths of reality with the inner eye of the heart because they are open to the depths of God revealed in fragile, finite humanity. Because what they see revealed remains concealed to those who are blind of heart, they love in a different way, they love without counting the cost, they love with all that they are. According to the "The Acts of the Process of Canonization," Clare was an example of this poor person, this mirror image of Christ, to her sisters. It is said that she washed the feet of her sisters, attended to their needs and strove to live in bonds of charity that would unite her community into the Body of Christ. Her hope for Agnes was transformation in Christ so that she could contemplate the humble presence of God in those around her and thus love in a new way, like the beloved. Clare's instruction is simple: Gaze upon the mirror of the cross each day and be transformed. Be honest and truthful. Do not be afraid to gaze upon your image. When you look into the mirror, what do you see?

QUESTIONS FOR REFLECTION

1. What does it mean to you to be created as an "image of God?" How do you grow in this image?

2. How can the cross help you to accept yourself and others? In what ways can the mirror of the cross be a positive tool for Christian growth?

3. How does the cross reveal to us authentic humanity? What are some ways we can foster relationship with the crucified Christ in our search for true humanity?

NOTES

1. See Regis J. Armstrong, "Clare of Assisi: The Mirror Mystic," *The Cord* 35 (1985), pp. 195–202.

2. Armstrong, "The Mirror Mystic," p. 197.

3. See, for example, Marguerite Porete, *The Mirror of Simple Souls,* Ellen L. Babinsky, trans. and intro., Robert E. Lerner, preface (New York: Paulist, 1993).

4. Himes, "The Sacrament of Creation," p. 43.

5. Bonaventure, *Hexaëmeron* (*Hex.*) 1.13 (VIII, 331). "Collations on the Six Days," volume V, *The Works of Saint Bonaventure,* José de Vinck, trans. (Paterson, N.J.: St. Anthony Guild Press, 1970), p. 8. The critical edition of Bonaventure's works is the *Opera Omnia,* PP. Collegii S. Bonaventurae, ed, 10 vols. (Quaracchi, 1882–1902). Latin texts are indicated by volume and page number in parentheses.

6. Clare of Assisi, "The Third Letter to Agnes of Prague" 12–13 (*Écrits,* 102), *Early Documents,* p. 45.

7. Miroslav Volf, *Exclusion and Embrace: A Theological Exploration of Identity, Otherness, and Reconciliation* (Nashville: Abingdon, 1996), p. 141.

8. Volf, *Exclusion and Embrace,* p. 141.

9. Volf, *Exclusion and Embrace,* p. 142.

10. Volf, *Exlcusion and Embrace,* p. 144.

11. For an explanation of embrace and not-understanding see Volf, *Exclusion and Embrace,* pp. 145–156.

12. See Francis of Assisi's "Admonition I" where he describes the Spirit's receptivity to the truth of Christ. He writes: "The Father dwells *in inaccessible light,* and *God is spirit,* and *no one has ever seen God.* Therefore He cannot be seen except in

the Spirit because *it is the Spirit that gives life; the flesh has nothing to offer.*... All those who saw the Lord Jesus according to the humanity, therefore, and did not see and believe according to the Spirit and the Divinity that He is the true Son of God were condemned." (*Adm* 1.5–8 in *FA:ED I*, p. 128).

[13] David Townsend, "The Passion of Dilawar of Yakubi," *National Catholic Reporter* (August 12, 2005), p. 22.

[14] Bonaventure, *Hex.* 2.32 (VIII, 341), p. 39.

[15] Clare of Assisi, "The Fourth Letter to Agnes of Prague," 19–23 (*Écrits*, 114), *Early Documents*, pp. 50–51.

[16] Michael D. Guinan, O.F.M., *The Franciscan Vision and the Gospel of John*, Series 4, Franciscan Heritage Series, Elise Saggau, ed. (New York: Franciscan Institute, 2006). See Part Two (the San Damiano Cross-Jesus' priestly garment), and Part Three (Francis and John 17).

[17] Clare of Assisi, "The Fourth Letter to Agnes of Prague," 15 (*Écrits*, 114), *Early Documents*, p. 50.

[18] Barbara Fiand, *Releasement: Spirituality for Ministry* (New York: Crossroad, 1987), p. 5.

[19] Fiand, *Releasement*, p. 5.

[20] Clare of Assisi, "The Third Letter to Agnes of Prague," 21 (*Écrits*, 104), *Early Documents*, p. 46.

[21] Clare of Assisi, "The Third Letter to Agnes of Prague," 22 (*Écrits*, 104), *Early Documents*, p. 46.

[22] Clare of Assisi, "The Third Letter to Agnes of Prague," 27–28 (*Écrits*, 106), *Early Documents*, p. 47.

Chapter Four

IMAGE AND IDENTITY

Along the streets of Venice there are shops that sell masks of many colors and shapes. A mask can hide a human face and allow us to take on the persona of another character—cats, birds, rabbits, queens, pirates, knights—these are just a few of the many masks we can wear. The Greek word for "mask," *prosÿpon*, is the root of the word *person*. A *prosÿpon* was a mask an actor wore in the theater to hide his own identity and to amplify the voice of the character.[1] The Latin word for "person," *persona*, is derived from the phrase *per sonare* or "to sound through." A person is one in whom there is a voice that "sounds through," just as when one wears a mask. The word *person*, therefore, connotes the idea of sounding through. To be a person is to ask: What kind of voice is sounding through my life? Is it my own voice or that of another? Do I wear a mask to hide my true identity and distort the voice that is truly mine? Clare raises the question of identity in her fourth letter to Agnes where she writes: "Gaze upon that mirror each day... and continually study your face within it."[2] By telling Agnes to study her face each day, Clare indicates that our true identity can only be found in the mirror of the cross.

The relationship between the mirror of the cross and the human face is an interesting one. The idea of the "face" not only connotes uniqueness and distinction, that which makes a person what she or he is, but it connotes form or expression since the face is what one sees. The face discloses the person in a particular way and therefore reflects one's personal identity or self-expression.[3] We identify one another by the face we see which bears a name. But does the face really disclose the person we claim to know? We have had probably at least one experience in life where a person we thought we knew surprised us by his or her actions. We thought we knew that person because we were familiar with his or her face but little did we know the voice sounding through them. Clare calls Agnes (and us) to authentic identity through the mirror of the cross. Who we are, the voice sounding within us, must be expressed on our face and in our actions. We are to come to a harmony of being and action, a peaceful acceptance of who we are inwardly and a freedom to express who we are outwardly.

In our contemporary culture, identity is in crisis. Among GenXers there is instability with regard to self-identity as they play in the sandbox of cyberspace. The complex age of cyberspace has given rise to "virtual reality" and "virtual identity." In the real world, many people are consumers who adorn themselves with the significance of brand items and take on the virtual identities these various logos personify.[4] The question of identity is not only challenged by virtual reality and consumerism but the very question of the *self* today is under revision. There is greater awareness today that we humans have emerged from an evolutionary process that has an ancient history. The idea of emergence underscores the fact that we are biologically linked, although not equal to, nonhuman creation and thus are situated in a web of life. While the word *relationship* has become a socially chic subject, it aptly connotes the basic morphology of created life, especially if we consider creation from a Trinitarian perspective. To describe the human person as relational is to say that the human person, like all of creation, is grounded in a Trinity of love. Contemporary anthropologists no longer view the human person as an autonomous unit or, in the words of Boethius, a *naturae rationabilis individua substantia* (an individual substance of a rational nature).[5] Rather, each beginning of finite, contingent life is an insertion into the web of life, so that the entire web changes with each new addition of created being or life. Each new creation is a cocreation; as we are created so too do we help create anew simply by entering the web of relationships. The human person, embedded in the web of life, is a pattern of relationships that influences the whole and is influenced by the whole, as relationships change. Scholars today describe the "self" not as a substantive part within an individual but as a pattern of relationships that is formed and influenced by the relationships themselves. The "true self" is not so much a precious unchanging core as a pulsating organic center.[6] In this respect, every human interaction that contributes to our sense of self in one way or another embodies relational power or a type of mutual power that allows for transformation of self.[7]

How does Clare's theology of the mirror contribute to our search for identity today? Although she was not a psychologist nor did she espouse an elaborate understanding of the human person, Clare was a deeply spiritual woman whose life was rooted in Scripture. She believed that we are created in the image of God and therefore find our true selves in God. She saw the cross as the source of our identity because here God comes to us on our own terms, that is, in our fragile human flesh. In the person of Jesus we see what it means to be an image of God. Perhaps if Clare was alive today her response to our identity crisis would be, "Why the fuss?" For she believed that our identity—who we are—is related to our image, what we are called to be. Each of us has a personal identity and each of us expresses the image in which we are created in a unique way. To know that image is to see it reflected in the mirror of the cross. She says to Agnes, "study your face in that mirror each day." Look and see who you are, what you are called to be, and where you have failed in love. Study, reflect, ponder your life as you behold the crucified Christ.

We are all familiar with the process of study. To study is not simply to read but to read slowly with concentration, to stop and reflect on certain ideas, to connect ideas, and to come to understanding and insight. To study one's face in the mirror of the cross is no different. It is not simply to look at the cross or give it a passing nod, as most of us do when we enter a church. It is rather to sit with the cross, to concentrate on the figure of the crucified Christ, to stop and reflect on the meaning of the Crucified as the love of God, to connect the meaning of the Crucified and our own lives, and to come to understand what we are and what we are called to be in our lives in view of the crucified Christ. For Clare, this process of study is integral to the level of love we call contemplation, the penetrating gaze that gets to the truth of reality. Contemplation begins when we can gaze—not merely look—on the mystery of God who is love enfleshed and nailed to a cross.

Clare urges Agnes to contemplate her image in the mirror of the cross. If contemplation is to study our face in the mirror of the cross, then contemplation is the way we achieve our true form as an image of God. To study our face in the cross is to ask who we are. In her own way Clare suggests that the self is not a substance separate from God but is created in relationship to God. Identity is uncovering the treasure within, the image of God in which we are created and by which we are in relationship with God. Identity, therefore, is the development of the self as an image of God; it is the creation of self precisely through relationship with God and with others. In Clare's words, it is finding that *"incomparable treasure hidden in the field* of the world and of the human heart."[8] The gaze on the mirror of the cross leads to contemplation of the crucified Spouse. In turn, this must lead us to plumb the depth of ourselves. The emergence of who we are in the mirror of the Crucified is expressed in what we become (our "face") and in the virtues we acquire inwardly and outwardly. As we come to be who we are called to be in relation to God (self-identity), God shows himself to the universe through his constant and continual creation of the self. God becomes the voice that sounds through our lives. The self that comes to be through a union with God in love is the self in which God is reflected, that is, the image of God. For Clare, contemplation is not a process or a step on a ladder to God. Rather it is integral to our identity and our development as the image of God. Contemplation is intertwined with transformation, as she writes in her third letter:

> And *transform* your entire being *into the image*
> of the Godhead Itself through contemplation.[9]

The enfleshment of God in our lives through contemplation and transformation is the renewal of Christ in the world.

Although Clare plumbs the heart of Christian identity in her letters to Agnes, we can briefly explore the question of identity through the lens of Francis' life as well. Francis was not magically transformed into a loving brother of creation. His was a constant effort toward conversion of heart, poverty, compassionate love and peace. Francis first encountered the crucified Christ in the San Damiano cross, and it was this image of God that spoke deeply to him about his own life. In one of the legends of Saint Francis the author describes Francis praying alone before the cross uttering the words, "Who are you, O Lord, and who am I?" The key to Francis' success (so to speak) was in acceptance of his identity, of who he was before God. Thomas Merton wrote that God makes things to be themselves and in being oneself lies the glory of God.[10] Just as the sunflowers and poppies of the Umbrian valley were saints gazing up into the face of God because they did nothing more than *be themselves*, so, too, Francis had to learn to be himself. Through the mirror of the cross, Francis grew into the self that God created him to be, a relational self, a self that could only be itself in true loving relationship with others. He became a family member of the household of creation because he accepted himself with his strengths and weaknesses, gifts and failings, and in this acceptance he found God. Finding God amid his own weaknesses, he found God in the weaknesses and frailties of others. Francis' life tells us that when we find God then we find ourselves, and when we find ourselves then we find the other as brother and sister because we discover that God lives in that person. When I posed the question of identity recently to a group of students, one student wrote, "I buy, therefore I am." How sad to think that personal identity is linked to what we materially possess. But in a consumer culture gone awry it is a reasonable answer. The further I am from my true self, Merton claimed, the self that God created me to be, the more wrapped up I am in my false self, the self I think I need to be and the one that is farthest from God, indeed the one God knows nothing about because God did not create it. This self, because it is in darkness, demands all my time and attention, turning me away from my true self embedded in the web of creation. When we relate to material things as the source of identity we can be sure that we are on the dangerous path toward nothingness.

It is no wonder today we seek to stand out with unique styles of clothes, hair, jewelry and whatever else may distinguish us. Our materialistic culture has promoted a crisis of identity by promoting images of what we are supposed to be or what we might be if we used certain products. Consumerism has nurtured a type of alienation where we are unable to accept who we are because we think we need to be something (or someone) else. We are so bombarded by images from the commercial media that we live with a multiplicity of identities, few or none of which are our own. I think the alienation of personhood and the crisis of identity today relates to rampant consumerism, Internet consumption and threadbare relationships. We are looking for a self without weakness and someone to love us despite our weaknesses. We are relational beings created for another but if we do not accept ourselves it is difficult to accept others. Francis' acceptance of the leper was, at the same time, an acceptance of his weak, limited self. As he accepted the leper by a kiss of the leper's hand, he accepted God in his life and in the life of the leper. In his *Testament* he said that after he was led among the lepers "what had seemed bitter was turned into sweetness of soul and body."[11] Francis discovered that the experience of God enfleshed transforms that which repulses us into a loving embrace. Recognizing the presence of God enfleshed in the leper impelled Francis toward a life of conversion in Christ. For Christ is the bridge that unites our alienated self to our true self, and our true self to others in which we find our completion.

We learn from Francis that the person who comes to know him or herself in God is the poor person, and one who is poor is free to love. Poverty for Francis, both material and spiritual poverty, enabled him to accept his radical dependency on God and others. He knew he was not the source of his own being and that every aspect of his life was gift. Even the "I" of his ego could not claim itself for itself. In his own way Francis knew the "I" comes from God and belongs to God. Poverty, therefore, enabled Francis to realize that he was a human person and as person, a relational being. He needed others if he was to be himself, and to be himself was to be dependent on others in whom God lives.

This dependency included not only humans but even the tiny creatures of Earth, flowers and worms, birds and rabbits. His vision of the universe, despite his physical blindness at the end of his life, was one of creation bound together in a luminous web of love. In this web Francis found his place as brother.

Clare calls us to a similar level of self-knowledge through the mirror of the cross. The mirror calls us to accountability as we begin to contemplate the image we see. It impels us to consider our behaviors as we place our mind, soul and heart in the mirror and embrace the image reflected there in a new way. We are drawn from an outside bodily awareness into a deeper experience of mutual indwelling through contemplative prayer. The "lens" of the mirror gives us a new way to view ourselves and to understand ourselves. Through this visible image, we are invited into a new relationship with ourselves and God. Christ is the mirror where God reveals himself to us and we are revealed to ourselves as we begin to see the truth of who we are—our identity—in the mirror of the cross. Gazing into the mirror of the cross, therefore, is both a *looking at* and a *receptivity to* God's self-giving love. We are to consider the actions of the "person" we see in the mirror (ourselves) with the actions of Christ who is the mirror itself. Clare encourages us to consider whether or not the way we act in the world "reflects" the virtues of Christ, the humility, poverty and charity of Christ. By gazing into the mirror we invite Christ into relationship with our intimate selves. As we see Christ in the mirror, and consider our face reflected in the face of Christ, we perceive what makes us a true reflection of Christ and what tarnishes the image. The power of Clare's mirror metaphor is that we cannot escape or deny the true image of ourselves. The mirror of the cross is perhaps the most concrete and visible statement of who we are.

In the same way, Clare knows that the Spirit searches the depths of the human heart through the mirror of the cross. The mirror of the Crucified tells us that we are most like God in this world through acts of love, especially when we love through suffering, poverty and humility. It also reveals what we do to God in this world—crucify him. In this mirror we see the greatness of the human capacity to love and the sorrow of human sinfulness. Contemplation is a penetrating truth of reality and when we contemplate the image in which we are created, we are led to the truth of who we are in God. The cross, therefore, indicates to us the true image of ourselves, and the image we need to gaze upon within ourselves—our own poverty, humility and suffering. To place ourselves in the mirror of the cross is to expose ourselves to the joys and sorrows of being human, the joy of God's all-embracing love, and the sorrow of seeing the Spouse "despised, struck, and scourged."[12] In the mirror of the cross we are to place our entire being—heart, mind and soul—and to *transform* your whole being *into the image* / of the Godhead Itself through contemplation."[13] Poverty, humility and charity are the "footprints of Christ" according to Clare and we are called to find these footprints within the depths of our own being. We must come to accept ourselves as we are with our strengths and weakness, gifts and failures. If we desire a deeper union with God, we must be prepared to face the pain and suffering of freeing ourselves from attachments that hinder deeper union with God. If we desire to live in our true identity, we must extinguish everything that is in the way of being like the crucified Christ, the image of God in whom we are created.

Clare had a real sense that death is the path to life. We might say that coming to our real identity means undergoing "little deaths" that peel away the layers of the false self that hide the true self within. To become who we truly are in God, we must die along the way, not once but many times—a lifetime of little deaths. Clare is convinced that the power of death is new life, the life of God, and in this life is the fullness of who we are created to be. She writes:

> If you suffer with Him, *you will reign with Him.*
> [If you] weep [with Him], you shall rejoice with Him;
> [If you] die with Him on the cross of tribulation,
>   you shall possess heavenly mansions *in the splendor of the saints.*[14]

The mirror of the cross means that our identity is hidden in the heart of God's love. Only in the cross can we see who we are and what we are called to be.

As we deepen our gaze in the mirror, we are drawn into the central mystery of human existence, our identity, each of us loved into being by God in a personal and unique way. Clare indicates that the gaze on the mirror is self-reflective. The God who is revealed in the crucified Christ is our image; it is what we look like when we can gaze into the mirror and accept ourselves and our capacity to love.[15] The more we contemplate Christ (by gazing upon the Crucified), the more we discover our identity, the person God created and called to be from all eternity. Each of us has an irreproducible "thisness," a certain personal and unique distinction that no one else can equally share. In this distinction lies the power of God to reveal himself in a new way, in our own personal and individual selves, despite our shortcomings, failings, weaknesses and limitations. From all eternity God has desired each of us, in a unique way, to be his glory and his eternal human face. God has desired our bodies with our own unique hands and feet to be his dwelling place. God desires to incarnate himself anew in our lives. It may seem unthinkable, but it is precisely when God can take on our flesh, when we make space for God to dwell in our lives, that we discover who we really are, and God's delight in us, in the continuing act of Incarnation.

For Clare, the cross is where we come to know God and ourselves in God. A life of poverty and humility, following the example of the crucified Christ, can lead us, like Agnes, to take hold of the treasure within the human heart which is the Word of God, in whom we are created. If the mirror of the cross helps us see the image of Christ reflected more and more in our own lives, then we must begin to consider how we are becoming like Christ in mind, soul and body. We may begin on the level of actions and behaviors, but we also must begin to consider the deeper aspects of who we are, what lies in our hearts, what occupies our minds, what inflames our souls' desires. That is why the gaze is self-reflective because the image we see in the crucified Christ is the image of our creation, and in this image is the basis of our identity. Contemplation is creative since it transforms the one who gazes in the mirror into a reflection of the image itself. The more we contemplate Christ, the more we discover and come to resemble the image of God. This image of God, brought to light in the one who gazes into the mirror of Christ, is expressed as a new "birth" of Christ in the believer. What do we mean by this "birth" of Christ? As we are drawn more deeply into relationship with God and ourselves in and through the mirror of the cross, we are asked to consider our lives in this world, whether or not we truly reflect Christ. It is one thing to look at our image in the cross and consider our behavior. It is another to consider whether the image we see is physically becoming like the person of Christ. To become like Christ is to embrace those parts of ourselves where darkness still lives in order to bring to them a vision of light and hope. It is a willingness to love in difficult situations, especially when we will not be loved in return.

While Clare's path entails a truthful relationship with God, it also involves our truthful relationships with our neighbors; it takes place in the context of community. In this respect, gazing upon the mirror of the Crucified is not an exclusive human-divine relationship, that is, a vertical relationship with a transcendent God. Rather, the divine is enfleshed in the other—immanent—so that to follow Christ is to follow the one who follows Christ, and to see ourselves in the mirror of the Crucified is to see ourselves in the faces of our suffering sisters or brothers. Clare's path is essentially Pauline (1 Corinthians 11: "Be imitators of me, as I am of Christ") and she directs Agnes to the fullness of being through relationship with a God who is enfleshed in fragile humanity, that is, the humanity of community.[16] For Clare, prayer without community cannot lead to the fullness of our self-identity, since it is in community that the mirror of our identity is reflected in the other, the neighbor whom we are called to love. Love transforms because love unites, and it is in loving our neighbor through compassion that we become more ourselves, and in becoming more ourselves, we become Christ.

This type of love does not ask for favors in return; it does not seek its own reward. Rather, it is the type of love that is willing to love for the sake of the other and thus to persevere through sufferings and trials—the unforgiving neighbor, the angry brother, the jealous sister. This is what Clare asks us to consider in the mirror—are we willing only to look on suffering from a distance or to shut it out from our lives or control it by whatever means possible? Or are we willing to enter more fully into the suffering of the other to know God and ourselves in a deeper way? When we live in contemplative union with God, we are able to taste the hidden sweetness of God's love in the fragile human flesh of another person. Discovering who we are—our identity—in the mirror of the cross empowers us to embrace ourselves despite our brokenness and flaws and, in turn, to embrace others with their brokenness and flaws. In the mirror of the cross we discover what it truly means to be loved by someone greater than ourselves. We discover the mystery of Christ, human and divine, the brother who shared life with us, who loved the Father unto death. We discover the power of God who raised him, and in him, all creation to new life. The mystery of Christ is our mystery. His image is our image. His life is our life. We are called to share in his power. We are to be the renewal of Christ in this world so that in all things God may be glorified. That is what we are created for, fragile vessels that we are: the glory of God. In the unique personal distinctions of our lives, our humdrum humanity, the power of God is revealed.

QUESTIONS FOR REFLECTION

1. How do you relate to the cross of Jesus Christ? Do you view it as a place of guilt and judgment or conversion and freedom?
2. What are some ways the cross can become your daily mirror? How can it help you find your true identity?
3. Do you relate to others as mirrors of Christ? Do relationships help you reflect on your own life?
4. Do you see yourself as a mirror of Christ for others to follow?

NOTES

[1] For a discussion on the meaning of "person" see Joseph W. Koterski, "Boethius and the Theological Origins of the Concept of Person," *American Catholic Philosophical Quarterly* (2004), pp. 205–206; Elizabeth Groppe notes that *prosÿpon* technically refers to the part of the head immediately below the cranium while the cognate term *prosÿpeion* "was used in reference to the mask worn by the actor on the Greek stage." See Elizabeth Groppe, "Creation *Ex Nihilo* and *Ex Amore*: Ontological Freedom in the Theologies of John Zizioulas and Catherine Mowry LaCugna," *Modern Theology* 21.3 (2005), p. 466.

[2] Clare of Assisi, "The Fourth Letter to Agnes of Prague," 15 (*Écrits*, 114), *Early Documents*, p. 50.

[3] The postmodern philosopher Emmanuel Levinas claims that the face of the genuine other should release us from all desire for totality and open us to a true sense of the infinite because inscribed in the face of the other is the trace of transcendence. One cannot grasp the other in knowledge, for the other is infinite and overflows in the totality of comprehension and of being. See Edith Wsychogrod, *Saints and Postmodernism: Revisioning Moral Philosophy* (Chicago: University of Chicago Press, 1990), p. 148; Robyn Horner, *Rethinking God as Gift: Marion, Derrida and the Limits of Phenomenology* (New York: Fordham University Press, 2001), pp. 64–66.

[4] D. Seiple, book review of "Consuming Faith: Integrating Who We Are with What We Buy," *Journal of American Academy of Religion* 73.2 (2005), p. 521.

[5] Koterski, "Theological Origins of the Concept of Person," p. 203.

[6] Jane Kopas, *Sacred Identity: Exploring a Theology of the Person* (Mahwah, N.J.: Paulist, 1994), p. 103.

[7] Kopas, *Sacred Identity*, p. 98.

[8] Clare of Assisi, "The Third Letter to Agnes of Prague," 7 (*Écrits*, 102), *Early Documents*, p. 45.

[9] Clare of Assisi, "The Third Letter to Agnes of Prague," 13 (*Écrits*, 102), *Early Documents*, p. 45.

[10] Merton, *New Seeds of Contemplation*, pp. 29–31.

[11] Francis of Assisi, "The Testamen," 3, in *FA:ED I*, p. 124.

[12] Clare of Assisi, "The Second Letter to Agnes of Prague," 20 (*Écrits*, 96). Clare writes: "Your Spouse . . . .was despised, struck, scourged untold times throughout his entire body, and then died amidst the sufferings of the cross." *Early Documents*, p. 42.

[13] Clare of Assisi, "The Third Letter to Agnes of Prague," 13 (*Écrits*, 102), p. 45.

[14] Clare of Assisi, "The Second Letter to Agnes of Prague" 21–22 (*Écrits*, 98), *Early Documents*, p. 42.

[15] See Ilia Delio, "Clare of Assisi: Beauty and Transformation," *Studies in Spirituality* 12 (2002), p. 75.

[16] For a discussion on the following of Christ in the context of community for Clare see Ilia Delio, "Mirrors and Footprints: Metaphors of Relationship in Clare of Assisi's Writings," *Studies in Spirituality* 10 (2000), pp. 67–181.

Chapter Five

CONTEMPLATION

There is a popular saying that goes around at least once in every family with a gleam of delight because it usually involves a significant change in a person. The saying is, "she (or he) fell in love." It is an interesting saying because *to fall* is to lose the ground of our security and enter into the unknown. According to science, we fall because of gravity. When we lose our balance, we are pulled by something greater than ourselves. To "fall in love" is to lose our balance, so to speak. It is to be pulled into the unknown by a force or gravity that impels us to leave behind our security and give ourselves over to the arms of another. Something greater than ourselves pulls us beyond ourselves to another. This pull is the gravity of love.

Contemplation for Clare begins by *falling in love*. It is being grasped by the power of God's love in the crucified Christ and giving ourselves over to that love. It is not some type of abstract spiritual union with God that ends on a note of spiritual bliss but a real personal encounter with the God of love in Jesus Christ. Gazing upon the crucified Christ causes us to lose our balance and be caught up in the divine embrace of love. Clare describes contemplation in the same context as personal transformation. We cannot contemplate God, she indicates, unless we are on the path of transformation. We contemplate God as we are transformed in God or, we might say, "we are conformed as we are transformed" in God. In her third letter to Agnes she writes:

> Place your mind before the mirror of eternity!
> Place your soul *in the brilliance of glory!*
> Place your heart *in the figure of the* divine *substance!*
> And *transform* your entire being *into the image*
> of the Godhead Itself through contemplation.[1]

Although the word *contemplation* literally means "one in mind with," for Clare the mind cannot be separated from the soul or from the heart. Contemplation, therefore, is of the mind, soul and heart and is a deepening of love through transformation in the beloved. Transformation is the basis of contemplation because only when the mind, soul and heart are open to the experience of God, touched by the grace of divine love, can one begin to contemplate God. Such change does not take place in isolation but in the encounter with God, as God comes to us in the person of Christ. Contemplation, therefore, is relational. It is the encounter with God as God appears to us in the ordinary flesh of our humanity and in creation. It is the fruit of the poor person who gazes on the poor crucified Christ and who sees in that poverty the brilliance of divine splendor. Contemplation is not a matter of self-reflection nor does it require a flight from the world. It is not a privilege of the cloistered monk or nun nor does it require certain traits. It not a genetic predisposition nor is it an esoteric experience. Contemplation means the ability to gaze on weak humanity and see there the presence of God, and to unite with what one sees.

Christianity is a sacramental religion, an outward sign of invisible grace. God is revealed to us and yet God is concealed in the humble signs of our creation. Too often we try to rationalize God and seek God in the brackets of our minds. Yet the type of contemplation that Clare proposes is of the heart; it is seeing God in ordinary reality. Francis used the word *contemplate* to describe the hidden presence of God in the humanity of Christ. In his first Admonition on the Body of Christ he wrote:

> [A]s they saw only His flesh [by means of their bodily sight], yet believed that He was God as they contemplated Him with their spiritual eyes, ...as we see bread and wine with our bodily eyes, see and firmly believe that they are His most holy Body and Blood living and true.[2]

Contemplation for Francis means to see God in Christ with the eyes of the spirit or to see the divine in the human through spiritual vision. For

Francis it is the humanity of Christ that enables one to see God with the "eyes of the spirit." The humility of God is such that God hides under an ordinary piece of bread, ordinary humanity, ordinary creation. "Look," he says, "at the humility of God!"[3] For Francis and Clare contemplation is not an intellectual exercise; it is a depth of vision, a penetrating gaze that gets to the heart of reality. We might say that the depth of something does not indicate that "behind" the phenomenon something else is waiting to appear, but that the very appearance of the phenomenon—as a way of being—reveals a depth. Contemplation is a way of seeing the depth of something that leads to union with what one sees. It de-centers by taking us out of ourselves and into the other by way of seeing; it is "horizontally ecstatic."[4] In seeing, we enter into the mystery and become united with what we see.

To contemplate one must first be able to gaze, not to stare at something or merely see with the physical eye, but to penetrate with the heart what is ordinarily missed by the eye. The eye of the heart must be opened by grace, enlightened by knowledge and strengthened by love. For Clare, the eye of the heart learns to see rightly in the mirror of the cross. Here, she indicates, one learns to contemplate by finding the truth of who we are in relation to the incarnate Word of God and incarnating that Word in our own lives. She tells Agnes to "totally love Him / Who gave Himself totally for [her] love."[5] The progression of prayer that leads to contemplation begins with the gaze on the crucified Christ and continues to penetrate the depths of this reality until the margins of the cross, poverty and humility, give way to the heart of charity which is hidden in the suffering heart of Christ. The movement toward contemplation is from outside to inside. It begins with the gaze of the beloved on the cross which leads to internalization of the Spirit that joins us to Christ. We are drawn into the mystery of God hidden in Christ. For Clare, the path to contemplation is linked with the experience of fierce suffering, an experience of having to die. She tells Agnes that she is to "die with him on the cross of tribulation." In some way, we must experience a cleansing and purging of all that is not of God in order to live wholly centered in God. God becomes the dwelling place or cocoon in which the old person dies and a new person emerges, just as the worm in the cocoon is transformed into the butterfly. Once a soul is dead to itself and its attachments, it breaks forth from the cocoon transformed. When someone has been purified intensely, the Beloved is experienced as the one:

> Whose affection excites
> Whose contemplation refreshes,
> Whose kindness fulfills,
> Whose delight replenishes.[6]

We no longer live by our own strength but by the Spirit of Christ who works in us. For Clare, contemplation is entering a new place of refuge, the dwelling place of God's love.

As a deepening of love, contemplation is a continuous action, an ongoing transformation, since nothing is more liberating and active than love. This love not only enables one like Agnes to see more clearly and deeply into the depths of the Spouse's love for her, but to feel[7] and taste the hidden sweetness of God.[8] The contemplative not only sees the depth of things but the vision itself leads to a type of "felt-love," to compassion. Contemplation awakens the senses and brings them to a new level of openness to God. We see differently, hear differently, taste new things and touch the presence of God in what others perceive as secular reality. The contemplative realizes that there is nothing profane for those who know how to see,[9] for the whole world is charged with the grandeur of God.

Clare understands that this new level of the senses, this deep penetrating vision of sacred reality, cannot take place apart from transformation in the beloved, and transformation cannot take place without continuously gazing into the mirror of the cross. Her idea of contemplation is not intellectual or speculative but it is an indwelling in love. The one who contemplates God is the one whose heart is centered in God. But to come to this place of centeredness, this heart full of love dwelling in God, we must gaze into the mirror of the cross and see there the joys and sorrows of being human, the joy of God's all-embracing love and the sorrow of seeing the Spouse "despised, struck, and scourged."[10] Clare indicates that we are to place our entire being—heart, mind, and soul—in the mirror of the cross and to *"transform* [our] entire being *into the image* / of the Godhead Itself."[11] This dwelling in God by which we are transformed into the image of God means that we remain with God, especially in times of suffering, so that fidelity to God (as God is faithful to us) leads to immense longing and ever-deepening love.

Francis of Assisi was a contemplative. "In all the poor," Bonaventure wrote, "that most Christian poor man also saw before him / a portrait of Christ."[12] The story of Greccio, where Francis celebrated the birth of Jesus, indicated that Francis saw more than a mere child in a manger since, according to the sources, he did not place a child in the manger when he reenacted the Christmas scene.[13] Rather, he had an altar constructed over the manger and a Mass celebrated, calling to mind the wonder of the Incarnation. With his heart aflame with love and his eyes streaming with tears, he considered the overflowing goodness of God poured out for us in the birth of Jesus and in the beauty of creation. The birth of Jesus was not an event of the past for Francis but a living reality of God's abiding presence in creation. God is not an abstract concept but a living reality of love, and it is this love which Francis discovered at the heart of the Incarnation. In Bonaventure's view one who knows Christ knows this love, and one who knows this love knows each element of creation as the expression of this love. What Francis came to perceive in the persons he met and in the things of creation is that each person or thing expresses the love of God and, as such, expresses Christ, for Christ is the love of God made visible in creation. In this way, the contemplative heart of Francis touched the contemplative heart of God through the heart of Christ. The whole of creation became for him a living icon of Christ, as Bonaventure wrote:

> Aroused by everything to divine love,
> he *rejoiced* in all the *works of the Lord's hands*
> and through their delightful display

he rose into their life-giving reason and cause.
In beautiful things he contuited Beauty itself
and through the footprints impressed in things
he followed his Beloved everywhere,
out of them all making for himself *a ladder*
through which he could climb up to lay hold of him
who is utterly desirable.[14]

The power of contemplative vision for Francis was, at the same time, a desire for God. His contemplation of creation was not merely a passive seeing but a deep penetrating gaze into the truth of the other. His continuous desire for God led him to realize that each creature is uniquely loved into being by God. He embraced each God-centered creature as if embracing Christ himself for, indeed, each spoke to him of the presence of Christ. In this way, the divine gift of God's goodness was made visible in the disfigured flesh of the leper and the tiny things of creation. Everything led Francis to embrace the beloved, Christ, for everything in some way expressed the Word of God.

Francis' way of contemplation is encapsulated in Clare's directive to Agnes to "Gaze upon that mirror each day...[and] contemplate the ineffable charity that led Him to suffer on the wood of the Cross."[15] Contemplation is not an end in itself for Clare but a path of union that must ultimately lead to action because to see God is to love God, and to love is to act. It is a demanding type of vision because if we really see the truth of God hidden in fragile flesh, how can we turn away? Are we not impelled to reach out and touch this God we so desire? Thus, she says to Agnes "let yourself be inflamed more strongly with the fervor of charity."[16] Contemplation, inflamed by love, is the basis of costly discipleship. For if we really see the depths of God revealed in persons or creatures who otherwise might be discarded, rejected or annihilated then we must act. We must do what we say we are—God-lovers. Clare realizes that such action is not superficial; rather it takes all that we are to unite with God in weak, fragile, suffering humanity. We may be rejected, imprisoned, excluded from community, ostracized by the church, but if we truly see then we must truly love. For Clare (as for Francis and Bonaventure) this love is the path of the crucified Christ.

Although contemplation leads to a new place of refuge in God, it also leads to being a Suffering Servant, one who is willing to lay down one's life for the sake of another. Contemplation can never be private, intellectual or purely spiritual because it is a matter of vision. It is not merely that we see the good and beautiful, avoiding the ugly or despicable. Rather we see the ugly and despicable *as* beautiful because God's love dwells precisely in weakness. Beauty appears in what is otherwise despised. Contemplation impels us to see things clearly and truthfully —for what they are and not what we expect them to be. The Gospels are filled with sayings of vision: "[I]f your eye is unhealthy, your whole body will be full of darkness" (Matthew 6:23). "But blessed are your eyes, for they see, and your ears, for they hear" (Matthew 13:16). This is why Jesus chastised the Pharisees, for they failed to see the goodness of God in their midst. "If you were blind, you would not have sin. But now that you say, 'We see,' your sin remains" (John 9:41). The person who contemplates God is one whose heart is turned toward God, for the path to contemplation removes the hardness of heart that blinds us in our pursuit of truth, beauty and goodness.

Although the traditional monastic path of contemplation leads to rest in God, Clare maintained that contemplation leads to action. Transformation and union with God does not mean retirement from ministry but rather new ways of being in the world. The more we are united with God, the more we come to act like God—not the God who we imagine is above us surrounded by angelic choirs of angels—but the God on the cross, the God who has revealed himself to us in the crucified Christ. After Francis of Assisi received the stigmata he did not withdraw into solitary retirement but returned to his ministry to lepers, burning with a desire to bring Christ's compassionate love to those in need. Both Clare and Francis show us that the one who seeks to contemplate God must learn to gaze upon the beloved crucified Spouse which means coming to dwell in the mystery of suffering and love. The one who seeks union with God is to become a servant of love.

Although the cross is central to Clare's spirituality, hers is not a spirituality of sin and guilt but rather one of freedom and transformation. The cross is the mirror of truth, where we come to see ourselves in our capacity to love and in our brokenness. An honest acceptance of who we are with our strengths and weaknesses is liberating, in Clare's view. Dwelling in the mirror of the crucified Christ leads us to that place of inner freedom, a freedom that is born of the joy of the Spirit and of union with the Spouse. Clare advises Agnes to study her face in the mirror each day so that she may be adorned with beautiful robes within and without, becoming transformed in union with the one she loves. To be adorned within and without is to "put on Christ" or to "re-present Christ," that is, transformation *is* imitation.

The relationship of the mirror and self-identity, which Clare describes in her fourth letter, corresponds to the method of gazing upon the Crucified which she describes in her second letter. A consistent gaze on the crucified Spouse ultimately leads to imitation, for when we cling to the crucified Spouse with all our heart we become an image of this Spouse in our own lives. Clare tells us that transformation or imitation of Christ cannot take place apart from self-identity or acceptance of ourselves in relation to God and our neighbor. The more we allow ourselves to be transformed by the Spirit of love, the more we become ourselves, and the more we become ourselves, the more we are like God. Each of us is created in a unique way to express the love of God in the world and to show the face of God to the world. The integral relationship between self-identity and imitation of Christ through contemplation is a path of transformation by which love draws forth the image in which we are created, an image which is made beautiful through the cross of suffering and love.

Clare's spiritual path is a spiral that goes to the depth of the human person's capacity for God and the capacity of God's love for the human person. Although Clare leaves only a few traces of insight to travel this path, Francis tells us more clearly that contemplation is the work of the Holy Spirit. Drawing upon the Gospel of John he writes: "The Father dwells *in inaccessible light*, and *God is spirit*, and *no one has ever seen God*. Therefore he cannot be seen except in the Spirit because *it is the Spirit that gives life; the flesh has nothing to offer*" (John 4:24, John 1:18).[17] The key to contemplation is the Spirit of the Lord. We must have the Spirit of

the Lord who joins us to Christ[18] to see into the depths of things.[19]
This, too, is Clare's idea. Openness to the Spirit means a dynamic relationship with God. In her second letter to Agnes she writes:

[M]ay you go forward
    securely, joyfully, and swiftly,

. . .

        in the pursuit of that perfection
        to which the Spirit of the Lord has called you.[20]

If we are joined to Christ, we have the Spirit of Christ and, thus, imitate Christ through the very expression of our "face"—the person God
created us to be. It is the Spirit who conforms us to Christ and enables
us to see the depths of God hidden in creation, "for the Spirit searches
everything, even the depths of God" (1 Corinthians 2:10). The link
between contemplation and transformation for Clare means that as we
come to a deeper truth of ourselves in relation to God we are filled with
the Spirit of God. It is the Spirit that allows us to see with the heart and
to contemplate the other with a penetrating gaze. In light of this relationship Clare writes:

Therefore,
    that Mirror,
        suspended on the wood of the Cross,
        urged those who passed by to consider, saying:
            "All you who pass by the way,
                look and see if there is any suffering
                like my suffering!"[21]

It is difficult to see another person's suffering if we have not come
to terms with our own suffering. We cannot see clearly the truth of
the other if we have not first seen clearly the truth of ourselves. The
relationship between "seeing" and "becoming" is governed by truth
and love. Honest acceptance of self and a real ability to love shapes
what we become. As we see the sufferings of Christ, so we are to
love: "From this moment, then, O Queen of our heavenly King, let

yourself be inflamed more strongly with the fervor of charity."[22] What Clare suggests is that contemplation is not a preliminary step to transformation or imitation but rather that we must strive to be transformed in Christ in order to contemplate the truth (depths) of Christ. Contemplation deepens as we continue to be transformed in Christ by coming to the truth of who we are in God.

The path to contemplation, therefore, begins with an acceptance of God's love in Christ, followed by a continuous gaze into the truth of this love, which should lead to a growth in self-identity in relation to God. Only one who is poor can gaze long enough to become inwardly free to be joined with Christ. The gift of the Spirit is the fruit of poverty which makes us inwardly free and open to accept the embrace of God's love in the embrace of the crucified Christ. The freedom that arises from poverty is not independence or autonomy but the freedom of the Spirit who not only joins us to Christ but enables us to gaze into the heart of Christ. If we "put on Christ" in our own life and see the suffering of Christ in our own life can then see Christ in the other and ultimately love like Christ. Gazing upon the crucified love of God impels us to assume the form of crucified love in our own lives.

Clare's way of contemplation is central to relationship with God. It is not the goal but the means of union and transformation. Without contemplation, transformation is not possible, and without transformation, the Body of Christ cannot grow. She therefore asks Agnes (and us) to dwell in the love of the crucified Christ, to center our hearts on a God who is unafraid to love what is weak and fragile and to imitate this love. To see, to love and to become what we love is the fruit of contemplation which can only be realized when we accept the poverty of being human, and in this poverty, accept the call to union with God. The words of the book of Lamentations that Clare uses are the words of the contemplative heart: *"All you who pass by the way, / look and see if there is any suffering / like my suffering."* Do we really see the suffering of Christ or do we merely pass by and let Christ continue to hang on a cross?

Recently, a Protestant minister enrolled in one of my courses on Franciscan spirituality. We spent a considerable amount of time discussing Clare's mirror mysticism and the implications of her mysticism for Christian life. Clare's spirituality made a deep impression on this young man. He told me that toward the end of the semester, around Thanksgiving, his mother came to visit him. He had not talked to her for several years and apparently had an estranged relationship with her. Having reflected on Clare's mirror of the cross, however, he began to see his mother in a new light. Instead of seeing a woman who had abandoned and abused him, he saw in her the figure of the crucified Christ, and what he saw impelled him to act with compassion. Before Clare, he said, he would have quickly ushered his mother out the door to the next bus bound for a long ride. But after reflecting on Clare and the mirror of the cross, he recognized the presence of the Crucified not only in his mother but within himself as well. While he saw his mother crucified by weakness and fragility, he saw himself crucified by the demons of his past, preventing him from loving her. So instead of pushing her out the door, he took her shopping for new clothes, drove her back to her assisted-living facility, saw that her room was decorated and cleaned, and that proper care would be ensured for her. Through the outstretched figure of the crucified Christ, love was restored between a mother and a son, because the son was able to contemplate the hidden presence of God in his mother and transcend his own limitations in his desire to love.

The path to God through contemplative vision for Clare takes seriously the outrageous love of God visible in the scandal of the cross. What we in our own time consider absurd—fragility, weakness, suffering and death—Clare, like many women mystics of her time, understood as the ensured path into divine love. The key to uncovering this love hidden in the field of the human heart is contemplation. For Clare, as for Francis, contemplation means looking upon the Earth while seeing the things of heaven.[23] It means seeing things for what they truly are, even in their weakness and brokenness, and not what we project onto them or want them to be. Her path of contemplation impels us to ask, What do we see as we travel the Earth? What are we looking for when we go about in the world? Clare reminds us that contemplation is the vision of a heart centered in Christ. Unless we can see God concealed in the fragility of our created world and love the God we see, our blindness remains and the world persists in darkness. Like the disciples on the road to Emmaus we foolishly ask, "Have you not heard? Did you not see?" Never realizing all the while that Christ is in our midst.

QUESTIONS FOR REFLECTION

1. How is contemplation integral to your daily vision of the world?
2. Does the cross play a central role in your desire for contemplation?
3. How do you understand the relationship between contemplation and transformation?
4. In what ways do you nurture a life of contemplation?

NOTES

[1] Clare of Assisi, "The Third Letter to Agnes of Prague," 12–13 (*Écrits*, 102), *Early Documents*, p. 45.

[2] Francis of Assisi, "Admonition I," in *FA:ED I*, p. 129.

[3] Francis of Assisi, "A Letter to the Entire Order," 27 in *FA:ED I*, p. 118.

[4] Michael Blastic, "Contemplation and Compassion: A Franciscan Ministerial Spirituality" in *Spirit and Life: A Journal of Contemporary Franciscanism*, volume 7, Anthony Carozzo, Vincent Cushing, Kenneth Himes, eds. (New York: Franciscan Institute, 1997), p. 168.

[5] Clare of Assisi, "The Third Letter to Agnes of Prague," 15 (*Écrits*, 104). "*illum totaliter diligas, qui se totum pro tua dilectione donavit.*" *Early Documents*, p. 46.

[6] Clare of Assisi, "The Fourth Letter to Agnes of Prague," 11–12 (*Écrits*, 112), *Early Documents*, p. 50.

[7] Clare of Assisi, "The Third Letter to Agnes of Prague," 14 (*Écrits*, 102). Clare writes: "So that you too may feel what His friends feel / as they taste *the hidden sweetness* / [of] God." *Early Documents*, p. 45.

[8] Clare of Assisi, "The Third Letter to Agnes of Prague," 14 (*Écrits*, 102), *Early Documents*, p. 45.

[9] This is the insight of the Jesuit scientist and mystic Pierre Teilhard de Chardin. See his *The Divine Milieu: An Essay on the Interior Life*, William Collins, trans. (New York: Harper and Row, 1965), p. 66.

[10] Clare of Assisi, "The Second Letter to Agnes of Prague," 20 (*Écrits*, 96). Clare writes: "Your Spouse...was despised, struck, scourged untold times throughout His entire body, and then died amid the suffering of the Cross." *Early Documents*, p. 42.

[11] Clare of Assisi, "The Third Letter to Agnes of Prague," 12–13 (*Écrits*, 102), *Early Documents*, p. 45.

[12] Bonaventure, "The Major Legend of Francis," 8.5 in *FA:ED II*, p. 589.

[13] For the story of Greccio, see "The Life of Saint Francis of Assisi," by Thomas of Celano in *FA:ED I*, pp. 254–257.

[14] Bonaventure, "Major Legend of Saint Francis," 9.1 in *FA:ED II*, pp. 596–597.

[15] Clare of Assisi, "The Fourth Letter to Agnes of Prague," 23 (*Écrits*, 114), *Early Documents*, pp. 50–51.

[16] Clare of Assisi, "The Fourth Letter to Agnes of Prague," 27 (*Écrits*, 116), *Early Documents*, p. 51.

[17] Francis of Assisi, "Admonition I," 5–6 in *FA:ED I*, p. 128.

[18] Again, Francis gave primacy to the Spirit of the Lord as the one who makes life in Christ possible. In his "Later Admonition and Exhortation" he wrote: "We are spouses when the faithful soul united by the Holy Spirit to our Lord Jesus Christ." See his "Later Admonition and Exhortation," 51 in *FA:ED I*, p. 49.

[19] The notion of penetrating vision is distinctive of Franciscan contemplation. Bonaventure used the term *contuition* to describe this penetrating vision which sees a thing in itself and in its relation to God. For a definition of *contuition* see Ilia Delio, *Simply Bonaventure*, p. 199.

[20] Clare of Assisi, "The Second Letter to Agnes of Prague," 13–14 (*Écrits*, 94), *Early Documents*, p. 41.

[21] Clare of Assisi, "The Fourth Letter to Agnes of Prague," 25 (*Écrits*, 114), *Early Documents*, p. 51.

[22] Clare of Assisi, "The Fourth Letter to Agnes of Prague" 27 (*Écrits*, 116), *Early Documents*, p. 51.

[23] See Francis' "Admonition XVI" on "Cleanness of Heart" where he wrote, "the truly clean of heart are those who look down upon earthly things, seek those of heaven, and, with a clean heart and spirit, never cease adoring and seeing the Lord God living and true." *FA:ED I*, p. 134.

Chapter Six

TRANSFORMATION

The genius of the saints is that they are not complacent or lulled by mediocrity. Rarely do the saints settle for anything less than the ultimate—union with God. Clare is no exception. Her strong personality shines through her letters with an inner conviction. She strives not only for union with God but for transformation. At least that is what she writes to Agnes,

> And *transform* your entire being *into the image*
> of the Godhead Itself through contemplation.[1]

She could have been less ambitious and tell Agnes something like "strive to enjoy each day" or "strive to show an act of kindness to those you meet." But Clare aims for the personal, direct, ultimate goal—transformation—which can only take place through contemplation. Unless we can "see ourselves" in God and God in us and in our neighbors, we really cannot dwell in the love of God which is the heart of contemplation. Transformation is related to contemplation because contemplation is dwelling in love, and real love is transformative. Love transforms, Bonaventure wrote, because love unites. Love changes the lover into the likeness of the beloved because true love transcends itself in the act of completion which takes place in relation to the other. Anyone who has seen a couple married for more than fifty years has probably witnessed a type of transformation whereby one partner is so attuned to the other, they move in harmony, if not simultaneously. I once knew a holy priest by the name of Walter Cieszak who endured an incredible struggle to remain faithful to God despite imprisonment and exile in Siberia. When I eventually met him in Bronx, New York, a year before he died, I knew I was in the presence of a person transformed by love. When he talked about God, a light radiated from his clear blue eyes. I believe I saw the face of God on the face of Walter Cieszak.

The word *transformation* is not part of our everyday vocabulary, so to understand why it is important to Clare's spiritual path we need to ask, What does it mean to "transform your being into the image of the Godhead"? The word *form* refers to a concrete expression of an inner content (or image). Form connotes shape, size, appearance and other characteristics which express matter or, we might say, inner being. The way something appears is its form. A cross, for example, may be composed of metal, wood or iron—that is its content or matter. But it is shaped by two bars perpendicular to each other—that is its form. To *trans*–form is to change the appearance or shape of something, from one expression to another. For example, if an iron cross is melted down, it could become a horseshoe. The matter would remain the same (it would still be iron) but the form would change. When we apply these philosophical categories of "form" and "matter" to the human person, we have something a bit more complex than a horseshoe but the idea that form can change is similar. Clare's directive to Agnes, to transform her being into the image of the Godhead, is another way of saying "be transformed into the one you love." Be changed—not in little ways but in a big way—the way of being a person. Let the life of God be your life. Let the face of God be your face. Become a new incarnation of the Word. Let Jesus Christ live in you. You will not change the genetic makeup of who you are but when the power of God's grace is at work in you, when love seizes your heart, you will express yourself in a new way, the way of love.

Clare's language of transformation is expressed in the language of imitation. She says to Agnes, "gaze on him...as you desire to imitate him." The key is desire. Do we *desire* to be transformed or are we content with our present form? It is not unusual to hear people say, "I wish I could be..." or, "I wish I was..." Are these not types of desire for transformation? Do they not express a discontentment with our present form? Clare says to Agnes that love is the real desire of the human heart and when we can attain a level of transcendent love (a type of love that goes beyond our immediate self-gratification) we will become perhaps what we always wanted to be, a human being fully alive.

The place of transformation for Clare is the person of the crucified Christ. Dwelling in love can change us. The gaze on the crucified Christ leads to the image of the crucified Christ becoming the form of one's life. Agnes is to leave behind her noble, aristocratic ways and become like her Spouse, crucified in love. This must have been quite a challenge for a woman who was destined to be a queen. "Gaze daily upon the mirror of the cross," Clare writes to Agnes. How is it possible that a suffering, crucified figure on a cross can be the object of our heart's desire and the center of transformative love? Does this not defy every Western cultural claim to life, beauty, joy and happiness? Yet, Clare is not promoting superficial piety. In our contemporary jargon, she "gets it," she understands the meaning of the cross. She does not understand the cross according to scientific, rational knowledge, as if she might have "figured out" the cross or solved its mystery like a puzzle. Rather, she understands it with her heart. Gazing upon the cross leads to that penetrating insight where the mind discovers its limits and yields to the heart. Knowledge may take us to the threshold of God but love enters into the mystery. Clare, like many of the saints, understood the power of God in the midst of weak humanity. She, like other saints, realized that *only* God can bring forth life from death. As Paul states, "If Christ has not been raised, your faith is futile and you are still in your sins" (1 Corinthians 15:17). Clare's insight into the power of God in the midst of suffering and death turns her heart toward Christ crucified in whom she sees the promise of life:

> O holy poverty,
>> God promises the kingdom of heaven
>
> . . .
>
>> to those who possess and desire you![2]

The knowledge of God's power in the midst of suffering and death gives Clare an inner conviction that the crucified Christ is the way to the fullness of life, as she writes to Agnes:

If you suffer with Him, *you will reign with Him.*

...

> [If you] die with Him on the cross of tribulation,
> you shall possess heavenly mansions *in the splendor of the saints.*[3]

She is not advocating suffering; rather, she is saying to Agnes, *if you truly believe in the power of God, if you have faith the size of a mustard seed, if you throw yourself into the arms of infinite love, then you will not fear the cross, you will not be afraid to suffer and die because in God death does not exist, only life.* Those who avoid the cross will die because without God, life is finite and limited. However, those who choose to take up the cross will live because God has shown the power of his love by transforming suffering and death into life. One who dwells in God dwells in love and one who dwells in love is fully alive! That is why Christ crucified is the way into God because he is the way into love, as Bonaventure wrote: "There is no other path than through the burning love of the Crucified."[4]

Although Clare sought a unity with God through contemplation of the crucified Spouse, union was not the goal of relationship with God; rather, the goal was imitation, or we might say, putting on Christ in one's life. The gaze on the crucified Spouse is to lead to imitation of the Spouse, not a literal mimicking of Christ, but becoming an image of the beloved through transformation. For Clare, imitation through contemplation takes place when we come to the truth of who we are in the mirror of the cross. She advises Agnes to "study her face in the mirror each day" so that she may be "adorned with beautiful robes within and without," becoming transformed in union with the one she loves. As we gaze upon the Crucified, we are to come to a deeper level of self-knowledge or identity in relation to God. This new level of knowledge should inform the heart in a new way so that the "old person" eventually dies and gives birth to the new person, the "Christic person," who has our face.

In Clare's view, daily gazing on the crucified Spouse ultimately leads to imitation, for when we cling to the crucified Spouse with all our heart we become like the Spouse in love, an image of the Crucified in our own lives. What Clare indicates is that transformation or imitation of Christ cannot take place apart from self-identity or acceptance of one's self in relation to God. Each of us is created in a unique way to express the love of God in the world and to show the face of God to the world. The integral relationship between self-identity and imitation of Christ through contemplation is a path of transformation by which love draws forth the image in which we are created, an image which is made beautiful through the cross of suffering and love. As we come to a deeper truth of ourselves in God, we are filled with the Spirit of God. It is the Spirit that allows us to contemplate the crucified Christ on the cross by a penetrating gaze in such a way that we can see the love of God hidden in otherwise fragile humanity.

There is no doubt that Clare's direction to Agnes, to become an image of Christ by imitating Christ, was quite bold for her time since the idea that women could represent God was a source of contention among many medieval writers. In the Middle Ages, women were considered inferior to men because they were associated with what is physical, weak and corruptible. Women were seen as the source of sin and as secondary images of God. The idea that women's souls were deficient, especially in the faculty of reason, is attributed to Aristotle who associated women above all with matter. Because women were defined through their bodies alone, they were not capable of truly being an image of God.[5]

Although the secondary status of medieval women was a given, Clare did not view her gender as inferior or incomplete. Rather, she saw herself as an image of God and capable of union with God because the Word became flesh and she herself was flesh. The bodiliness of the incarnate crucified Word opened up for her a path into divine love and revealed to her the meaning of being the image of God. Thus, Clare held that everyone who follows Christ is called to put on Christ (see Galatians 3:27) and to be transformed in divine love.

Transformation requires real change in our lives. To "trans-form" our lives is another way of talking about conversion. Conversion does not mean today I am a sinner and tomorrow I will be a saint. Rather, it is an awareness of our weakness and our need for God, our desire for wholeness and our openness to grace. Conversion means that we are willing and free to change. Since we come from God, our incomplete lives today are destined to be complete in God tomorrow. How it will attain this completion depends on the choices we make. God desires our completion but will not accomplish it without us. By gazing on the mirror of the cross we are called to conversion which is an ongoing movement toward God in openness, freedom and grace. Conversion, like transformation, entails change, becoming other than what we already are or rather becoming what we are intended to be from all eternity, a new incarnation of the Word. This change cannot take place unless we become more conscious of our choices and how we are influenced by cultural, religious and political forces over which we have little control; more conscious of our poverty as human persons; more conscious of our neighbor in whom God lives; more conscious of the sacramental life of the church as a fountain of grace; more conscious that we are members of the Body of Christ. And this consciousness must influence our hearts because what flows from our hearts determines what we are, how we act, and what we will become through our actions.

Delir Brunelli points out, "Clare's contemplation has, in its own fiber, the dimension of witness, commitment, and the proclamation of the Gospel. Whoever is transformed in the mirror of Christ, by this fact alone, radiates and manifests his image."[6] What does this mean for us? Can we really manifest the crucified Christ in such a way that the presence of Christ becomes visibly expressed in our lives? Clare's answer is yes. We not only *can* do this, we are created to express the Word of God in our lives. In fact, without striving for such a goal, we remain incomplete and lost, ambivalent, restless and anxious. What Clare calls us to is not something other than what we are but rather what we truly are created to be—icons of Christ. Christ lives in us and becomes our life when we come to live our true identity (or self) in God. To put on Christ is to allow God to take root in our hearts and put on our flesh, not hiding God in the little pockets of our hearts (and thus not letting anyone know we are religious or being so privately religious that we refuse to talk about our beliefs) but rather allowing the grace of God to shine through in our lives—fragile and weak as they may be. Our lives become sacramental—not in a dramatic way, as if we were tattooed with divine stars,—but simply by becoming our vessels of grace—or as Mother Theresa often said, doing extraordinary acts of love in ordinary human ways. The contemporary writer Gil Bailie claims:

> "[T]he person is a natural sacrament inasmuch as a person always carries the constituting imprint of another, re-presenting a desire awakened by the other and turning the person toward Christ. By making this mimetic reality conscious, Christianity gives this natural sacrament of the person a religious significance, one that marks Christian subjectivity with its distinctive character."[7]

Francis of Assisi is a good example of a sacramental person, one who lived in the grace of conversion, contemplation and transformation. If we were to identify the central theme of Francis' way of life, it is the Incarnation. It is what defined his way of going about in the world. We can say that Francis was grasped by Christ, that is, by the God of overflowing goodness revealed in the human person of Jesus. His life became filled with Christ whom he encountered in the Scriptures, in the Eucharist, in his brothers and sisters and in the tiny creatures of creation. His biographer Thomas of Celano wrote that Francis was preoccupied with Jesus,

> He was always with Jesus:
> Jesus in his heart,
> Jesus in his mouth,
> Jesus in his ears,
> Jesus in his eyes,
> Jesus in his hands,
> he bore Jesus in his whole body.[8]

This "grasp" by God gave Francis a new outlook on the dignity of the human person, a new sense of creation as family and a new view of God as generous love.

What Francis discovered in Christ was the value of relationship. Because of Christ he realized first the power of God's love in his own life. Then he realized that God is related to each person in a unique and irreproducible way and, finally, that we are related to one another because each of us has our source in God. To know Christ is to know the hidden God of overflowing goodness among us.

Bonaventure describes the progress of Francis' life as a development of personhood, that is, a movement from a self-isolated subject to a self that is essentially open and related to the other. By experiencing God's love in the visible figure of the Crucified, Francis became a man of true relationship. He was able to turn away from self-concern and from the ego's grasp, and pass over into the other in whom he found the infinite goodness of God. Because of the mystery of Christ, Francis' personhood developed from a self-centered "I" to a relational self in need of a "Thou." The deeper he grew in relationship with Christ, the deeper he grew in relationship with others because he realized his "I" needed a "Thou." As Francis deepened his relationship with Christ, his neighbor became less outside him as object and more related to him as brother.

The example that most aptly describes this change in Francis is the leper. In his youth, Francis despised lepers and would turn away at the sight of them. However, after he encountered God's compassionate love in the crucified Christ, he had a change of heart. The expression of God's love in the self-emptying of the cross impressed Francis in such a way that what was loathsome to him, namely, the sight of lepers, became the object of his love. This conversion experience of Francis marked the beginning of his transformation which Bonaventure describes in view of the cross. At the beginning of his spiritual journey, Bonaventure indicates that the crucified Christ was "outside" Francis, unrelated to him in the same way the leper was unrelated to him. As Francis grew in knowledge and love, his relationship to Christ (and thus to the lepers) changed. He began to minister among the lepers, calling them his "Christian brothers." Bonaventure describes the transformation of Francis' life as a transformation in love, a visible expression of "the burning love of the Crucified Christ." Francis' transformed life attained its height on the mountain of La Verna where he went to fast and pray. There he had an experience of the Crucified that Bonaventure describes as an ecstatic experience of love. Francis was filled with a marvelous ardor:

> [T]hat he was to be totally transformed
> into the likeness of Christ crucified,
> not by the martyrdom of his flesh,
> but by the enkindling of his soul.[9]

Francis became a new visible sacrament of the Lord. Although the stigmata of Francis have received various interpretations in recent years,[10] still they indicate something dramatic about Francis' life and the way he lived in union with Christ. Francis attained such a profound level of transcendent love that he was considered "another Christ."

The centrality of Christ in Francis' life hinged on neither superficial piety nor mere devotion. Rather, he became "formed" in the Christ mystery. Bonaventure indicates that the more Francis entered into the mystery of Christ in his own life, the more he recognized Christ in the people and creatures around him. Francis saw Christ in the irreproducible uniqueness of each person and creature so that all things, each in its own way, led him to embrace Christ. God was not an abstract concept for Francis but a living reality of love, and it is this love which he discovered in the Incarnation and thus at the heart of the creation. In Bonaventure's view, one who knows Christ knows this love, and one who knows this love knows each thing of creation as the expression of this love. What Francis came to perceive in the persons he met and in the things of creation is that each person/thing expresses the love of God and as such expresses Christ, for Christ is the love of God made visible in creation. His deep love of Christ led him to contemplate the mystery of God in his own life, in the lives of others and in the world. As his life deepened in Christ, everything spoke to him of Christ and led him to embrace his beloved. Using the language of Clare, contemplation of the beloved for Francis led him to embrace the beloved, and in embracing the beloved he became like the beloved in love. According to Thomas of Celano he went about the world saying,

"The love of him who loved us greatly
is greatly to be loved."[11]

And love greatly he did. At the end of his life he came to appear like the Beloved he had so faithfully followed. Celano recounts the story of a friar who had a dream, after Francis' death, in which he could not distinguish Francis from Christ:

At the very same hour that evening the glorious father appeared to another brother of praiseworthy life, who was at that moment absorbed in prayer. He appeared to him clothed in a purple dalmatic and followed by an innumerable crowd of people. Several separated themselves from the crowd and said to that brother: *"Is this not Christ, brother?"* And he replied: *"It is he."* Others asked him again, saying: "Isn't this Saint Francis?" And the brother likewise replied that it was he. For it really seemed to that brother, and to the whole crowd, as if Christ and Saint Francis were one person.[12]

There is little reason to doubt that Francis' life became a mirror image of Christ. People saw in him a "Christ presence" that had a profound effect on others. We might say that the life of Christ was visibly renewed in Francis, and this presence of Christ impelled others to change their lives.

Clare herself was deeply inspired by the life of Francis. She felt bonded to him as a plant to its root and saw in him the example of Christ. In the *Testament*, attributed to Clare, it is written, "The Son of God has been made for us the *the Way* (cf. Jn 14:6) which our blessed father Francis, His true lover and imitator, has shown and taught us by word and example."[13] In her view, to contemplate Christ and be transformed is to bear witness to Christ and thus to allow the life of Christ to shine through the life of the believer. Christian life is about visible presence. We are not only to follow Christ but to give birth to Christ in our lives. Clare's spiritual path is a mystical one. It is a mysticism of motherhood because she not only seeks the hidden presence of God but asks that the love of God be brought to birth in our lives. She holds up Mary, the Mother of God, as the model of this mystical path, indicating to Agnes that she should "cling to His most sweet Mother who gave birth to a Son whom the heavens could not contain."[14] Clare sees the potential of the human person as one of making God present in our lives. In her third letter she states that the soul of a faithful person, like Mary, is greater than heaven itself, "since the heavens and the rest of creation cannot contain their Creator and only the faithful soul is his dwelling place and throne."[15] She emphasizes the capacity of the human soul to bear God. The one who is joined to Christ by the Spirit is one in whom the Trinity dwells. Poverty and humility make possible this indwelling of God in such a way that we, like Agnes, can ultimately come to possess God, insofar as a human person can possess God in this earthly life. She continues by saying:

> As the glorious Virgin of virgins carried [Him] materially, so you, too, *by following in* her *footprints* (cf. 1 Pet 2:21), especially [those] of poverty and humility, can, without any doubt, always carry Him spiritually in your chaste and virginal body, holding Him by Whom you and *all things are held together...* (Wis 1:7)[16]

What profound insight from a woman of deep prayer, that the Creator of all can be held within the finite space of the human heart! How can we possess God unless we are so intimately united with God that God's life becomes our life and our life is God's life? Clare calls us to enter into the mystery of bearing God in the womb of our hearts and giving birth to Christ in our lives. It is a spiritual ideal to which Francis himself aspired when he wrote: "[We are] mothers when we carry Him in our heart and body...and give Him birth through a holy activity."[17]

For Clare, as for Francis, the one who gives birth to Christ is so intimately joined to Christ as spouse (through the Holy Spirit) that ones shares in the sacred banquet of love. In her fourth letter she writes:

> Happy, indeed, is she
> > to whom it is given to share in this sacred banquet

so that she might cling with all her heart
to Him
> Whose beauty all the blessed hosts of heaven unceasingly
> admire.[18]

Clare's language of intimacy is graphic —to "cling" and "possess" is to come to such a union with Christ that the life of Christ is virtually inextricable from the life of the believer. To bear Christ in our lives is to be drenched with grace: His life becomes our life, his love becomes our love. Transformation is not so much a process or method but a redirection of our life's energy, the Spirit of life that we welcome into our lives, the Spirit that enlightens our minds and recreates our hearts as dwelling places of God. Poverty is the door to transformation. When we recognize our dependency on God, when we create a space within us to welcome God in our lives, and when the spiritual eye of the heart gazes on our own image in the mirror of the cross, then transformation is possible. Then we are free to be seized by God and to be transformed into God, not becoming divine by nature but allowing the divine to shine through our lives. This transformation means, for Clare, becoming like Mary, another *Theotokos* or God-bearer. The one who "bears God" gives witness to Christ because God takes on flesh anew in life of the faithful person. It is indeed good news when Christ is born anew.

QUESTIONS FOR REFLECTION

1. How are you attentive to transformation in your daily life?
2. How does the cross play a central role in your path to God? How is it the mirror of self-reflection and the place of transformation for you?
3. How do you understand the concepts "imitation," "image," and "crucified love" in your own life?
4. In what ways does Clare's "mysticism of motherhood" speak to you?

NOTES

[1] Clare of Assisi, "The Third Letter to Agnes of Prague," 13 (*Écrits*, 102), *Early Documents*, p. 45.

[2] Clare of Assisi, "The First Letter to Agnes of Prague," 16 (*Écrits*, 86), *Early Documents*, p. 36.

[3] Clare of Assisi, "The Second Letter to Agnes of Prague," 18–20 (*Écrits*, 96), *Early Documents*, p. 42.

[4] Bonaventure, prologue to the *Itinerarium* 3 (V, 295). *Bonaventure: The Soul's Journey into God, The Tree of Life, The Major Life of Saint Francis*, Ewert Cousins, trans. (New York: Paulist, 1978), p. 54.

[5] George H. Tavard, *Women in Christian Tradition* (South Bend, Ind.: Notre Dame, 1973), p. 115. See also Eleanor Commo McLaughlin, "Equality of Souls, Inequality of Sexes: Women in Medieval Theology," in *Women in Western Thought*, Martha Lee Osborne, ed. (New York: McGraw Hill, 1979), pp. 62–66.

[6] Delir Brunelli, " 'Contemplation in the Following of Jesus Christ': The Experience of Clare of Assisi," *The Cord* 52.4 (2002), p. 167.

[7] In a personal communication, Gil Bailie replied that the source of this quote is unknown. "I don't know when or where I used it," he said, "probably in an unpublished lecture."

[8] The Life of Saint Francis by Thomas of Celano," in *FA:ED I*, p.283.

[9] Bonaventure, "The Major Legend of Saint Francis," 13.3 in *FA: ED II*, p. 632.

[10] See for example Chiara Frugoni's chapter "The Stigmata: A Discovery, A Pious Story or an Invention" in *Francis of Assisi: A Life*, John Bowden, trans. (London: SCM, 1998), pp. 118–147. Frugoni critically examines the authenticity of the stigmata in light of the fact that it was not reported until after the death of Francis in 1226.

[11] "The Remembrance of the Desire of a Soul by Thomas of Celano," 148 in *FA:ED II*, p. 373.

[12] "The Remembrance of the Desire of a Soul by Thomas of Celano," 165 in *FA:ED II*, p. 389.

[13] Clare of Assisi, the *Testament*, 5 (*Écrits*, 167), *Early Documents*, pp. 56–57.

[14] Clare of Assisi, "The Third Letter to Agnes of Prague," 18 (*Écrits*, 104) *Early Documents*, p. 46.

[15] Clare of Assisi, "The Third Letter to Agnes of Prague," 21–22 (*Écrits*, 104), *Early Documents*, p. 46.

[16] Clare of Assisi, "The Third Letter to Agnes of Prague," 24–26 (*Écrits*, 106), *Early Documents*, p. 46.

[17] Francis of Assisi, "Later Admonition and Exhortation," 53 in *FA:ED I*, p. 49.

[18] Clare of Assisi, "The Fourth Letter to Agnes of Prague," 9 (*Écrits*, 112), *Early Documents*, p. 50.

Chapter Seven

EUCHARIST

In an age of post-modern spirituality where religion is associated with the institutional church and spirituality with inner conviction and feeling, the Eucharist has been relegated to devotion and personal piety. It has become a private encounter between the inner soul and Jesus as if the world is removed for a moment in time in the embrace of God. But the Eucharist was never meant to be a love affair in a private dining room. As the culminating point of Jesus' life, we might say, it is the most public expression of God's abiding presence. The Eucharist is not about a small wafer on a golden plate, it is about the Body and Blood of Christ and the body and blood of our lives.

Both Francis and Clare seem to have understood the meaning of Eucharist without ever really talking about it. Although Clare does not use the language of Eucharist in her letters to Agnes, the type of love that she describes is a eucharistic love, a love poured out for the sake of the other, which makes one a vital member of Christ's Body, the church. For Clare, the Body of Christ defines the church. She urged Agnes to pursue the path of eucharistic love because only in this way could she help rebuild the church by strengthening the Body of Christ through her own life. In her third letter to Agnes she wrote: "I consider you *a co-worker of God* Himself (cf. 1 Cor 3:9; Rm16:3) and a support of the weak members of His ineffable Body."[1] What remarkable insight from a woman who lived most of her life separated from the noisy world—that to live a eucharistic life is to become the Body of Christ in our own lives and to become vital participants in the life of the church. The Body of Christ and the church are not two separate realities but the single mystery of God's continued presence intertwined with our broken, sinful world.

Clare's thoroughly incarnational spirituality is rooted in the life of the church—not a perfect, spiritual church but a messy, human one that struggles with the mystery of Incarnation. In the Middle Ages, various heretical sects such as the Cathari broke from the church in the pursuit of spiritual perfection but Clare, like Francis, remained obedient to the church despite her struggle for an authentic Christian life. The spiritual conviction of Clare's eucharistic spirituality is woven like fine threads in her letters but it is centered on the Body of Christ. She is convinced that when the Body of Christ becomes the body of the believer, that is, when one is inflamed like Christ crucified with the fervor of charity, then one is willing to offer one's life for the sake of the gospel. In her view, the lover is to become, like the beloved, cruciform in love.

Clare's own expression of cruciform love is reflected in the defense of her monastery against the Saracens, as recounted in "The Acts of the Process of Canonization." According to the ninth witness, Sister Francesca, as the Saracens were approaching the monastery, the Body of Christ was brought to Clare who offered herself as a victim in defense of her sisters' lives and of the city itself. The witness states:

> [W]hen the Saracens entered the cloister of the said monastery, the Lady made them bring her to the entrance of the refectory and bring a small box where there was the Blessed Sacrament of the Body of our Lord Jesus Christ. Throwing herself prostrate on the ground in prayer, she begged with tears, saying among other things: "Lord, look upon these servants of yours, because I cannot protect them." Then the witness heard of voice of wonderful sweetness: "I will always defend you!" The Lady then prayed for the city, saying: "Lord, please defend the city as well!" The same voice resounded and said: "The city will endure many dangers, but it will be defended." Then the Lady turned to the sisters and told them: "Do not be afraid, because I am a hostage for you so that you will not suffer any harm now nor any other time as long as you wish to obey God's command-ments." Then the Saracens left in such a way that they did not do any harm or damage.[2]

This testimony is important not only for the holiness of Clare's life but for bearing witness to the importance of the Eucharist in her life. It is significant that, after the Body of Christ was brought to Clare, she prostrated herself in prayer and declared herself a hostage so that the sisters would not be harmed.[3] Like Christ, Clare was willing to lay down her life for the lives of her sisters. We find a similar spirit of cruciform love in Clare's desire to go to Morocco to endure martyrdom for love of the Lord, as the sixth witness in "The Acts of the Process of Canonization" described.[4]

The Eucharist as cruciform love is also evident in the life of Francis of Assisi. Thomas of Celano, following a Pauline theme, develops a relationship between Christ's crucified body and the body of Francis. Paul's notion of the Eucharist is, in part, a rejection of the Hellenic notion that commitment to the One (or God) implies a disdain for the body. According to Hellenic thought, commitment to the One or unity with God meant an erasure of difference, since the body was to be transcended or denied in the pursuit of spiritual perfection. As Miroslav Volf writes, the One in whom Paul seeks to locate the unity of all humanity is not disincarnate transcendence but the crucified and resurrected Jesus Christ. The principle of unity has a name, and the name designates a person with a body that has suffered on the cross.[5] All are made one body of God's children without regard to gender or race because of the cross (cf. Galatians 3:28). Paul writes: "Because there is one bread, we who are many are one body, for we all partake of the one bread" (1 Corinthians 10:17). The bread that Paul refers to is the crucified Body of Christ, the Body that has refused to remain a self-enclosed singularity, but has opened itself up so that others can freely partake of it.[6] Volf explains:

> The grounding of unity and universality in the scandalous *particularity of the suffering body of* God's Messiah is what makes Paul's thought structurally so profoundly different from the kinds of beliefs in the all-importance of the undifferentiated universal spirit that would make one "ashamed of being in the body."[7]

Far from being one against the many, the significance of Christ crucified is the self-giving of the one for the many. The crucified Messiah creates unity, therefore, by giving his own self. Because Christ unites different bodies into one Body through his suffering on the cross, it is the surrender of the Crucified through self-giving love that is the basis of true Christian community.

This understanding of the Body of Christ as the basis of unity plays out in Celano's life of Francis where the underlying theme of Eucharist is expressed in the relationship between the Body of Christ and the body of Francis. The Pauline notion of Eucharist as the crucified body of Christ is the background for the meaning of the stigmata of the mountain of La Verna. Celano describes the event as a visual event whereby Francis "saw *in the vision of God* a man, *having six wings like a seraph, standing over* him, *arms extended and feet joined*, affixed to a cross."[8] Francis was filled with a mixture of joy and sorrow as he tried to discern the meaning of the vision. According to Celano, the meaning of the vision was revealed in the body of Francis himself as he descended from the mountain marked with the wounds of Christ. Celano interprets the stigmata in light of the Pauline notion of spirit and flesh. True spirituality is the harmony of spirit and flesh. The use of the word *flesh (sarx)* in Paul does not refer to the body but rather all those things that stand opposed to God. Francis, conformed to the crucified Christ, became a truly spiritual person because:

> There was in him such harmony of flesh with spirit
> and such obedience that,
> as the spirit strove to reach all holiness,
> the flesh did not resist
> but even tried to run on ahead.[9]

We find a similar harmony in Clare, although she attains no visible stigmata nor are there biographical details to explain how she attained spiritual maturity. In the "Versified Legend of the Virgin Clare," however, the author devotes a long section to the "mortification of the flesh" indicating that Clare undertook a harsh ascetical life in an effort to subdue the "burdens of the flesh" in order to liberate the spirit to be for God.[10] Celano indicates that Francis' embrace of suffering enabled his spirit to be set free for God. Thus, it is in light of the wounded body of Francis that Celano described him as a truly spiritual person. He wrote:

> According to the laws of nature and the human condition *day by day* the body must *decay* though the *inner being is renewed*. So the precious *vessel* in which the heavenly *treasure was hidden* began to shatter all over and lose all its strength.... And so the *spirit* became *willing* in the *flesh that was weak.*[11]

For Celano, Francis' frail and weakened body became a source of spiritual strength—salvific—in the same way that Christ's crucified body became the source of healing and wholeness for the world. The spirit that flowed from the wounded body of Christ is the same spirit that flowed from the wounded body of Francis. Despite the fact that Francis' body was dying, he still maintained an inner desire to be with Christ for, as Celano said, "he had not yet *filled up in* his *flesh what was lacking in the sufferings of Christ.*"[12] Celano, therefore, saw Francis' wounded flesh as a participation in the sufferings of Christ for the redemptive completion of the world. In this way, Francis became the exemplar of the true Christian life because he was willing, like Christ, to suffer for the sake of reconciliation and peace. What makes Francis another Christ according to Celano is not his actions per se but the excess of love which bore itself out in his willingness to suffer like Christ. Again, we have no elaborate description of such love in Clare but it is evident in the testimonies of the Sisters given at "The Acts of the Process of Canonization." Many sisters recounted Clare's selfless love for others, including care of the sick and attentiveness to the needs of the community. The second witness at the "Process," for example, recounted Clare's profound humility by stating:

> Lady Clare...had marvelous humility and so looked down upon herself and that those tasks which she knew were more degrading she herself performed.
> She even cleaned the matresses [sic] of the sick sisters with her own hands....

More than this, the blessed Clare used to hand water to the sisters and, at night, covered them from the cold.[13]

We might say that love transformed the body of Clare and the body of Francis into crucified bodies in the same way that love transformed Jesus into the living Christ. As Celano writes, the love that ultimately forged Francis into Christ was

[T]he spring of radiant love
that filled his heart within
[and] gushed forth.[14]

This same love, I believe, was also in the heart of Clare. It is through the power of love that Francis and Clare, transformed in Christ, became other Christs for others to see and follow.

The power of love is the Spirit, for it is the Spirit sent by Christ who conforms us to Christ, not by erasing our identity but rather by shaping the persons we are into the vessels of love we are created to be. The Spirit sets us free in love to be for love, because the Spirit leads us to the truth of who we are in God in whom we find our freedom. Anything that does not lead to true freedom must be rejected as untrue. Thus, the gospel is a constant call to freedom, an invitation to shape our own lives rather than allow ourselves to be influenced by an imaginary world order or to have any code simply thrust upon us.[15] Francis was truly a free man because he lived in the power of the Spirit, and in this power of love he became the new life of Christ in the world. Jesus risen from the dead was alive in Francis. And the power of love that permeated Francis' life permeated the world around him. Francis' life had an impact on the world around him. Consider how many stories were written about him! The whole universe became more Christic because of Francis, moving forward toward its completion in God.

The love by which Francis' life became like burning incense is cruciform love because it is the love of the servant. It is the type of love that is willing to bend down and wash the feet of another. It is no secret that Francis and Clare described themselves as "servants" because they were not afraid to bend down and wash the feet of their brothers and sisters. In Clare's "Process of Canonization" the evidence of Clare's humility was repeatedly noted. The third witness, for example, said that:

> One time, while she was washing the feet of one of the serving sisters of the monastery, she turned to kiss her feet. The sister clumsily withdrew her foot and thus, while pulling it away, she hit the holy mother in the mouth with her foot. Nevertheless, because of her humility, Clare did not desist but kissed the sole of the foot of the servant.[16]

Michael Blastic claims that the image of Jesus as foot washer defines the role of authority for Francis and Clare. The eucharistic passage of the synoptic Gospels is translated into the washing of feet in the Gospel of John, indicating that the Eucharist involves a community of mutual service and worship.[17] Similarly, the Eucharist for Clare and Francis was not mere receptivity of the Body of Christ but living in the profound presence of God's indwelling love. It meant a contemplative gaze on the humility of God hidden in fragile humanity and transformation in this humble love. The lives of Francis and Clare show us that to live a eucharistic life is to respond to God in the generosity of love; thus, it is an activity, a way of being, that shapes relationships among brothers and sisters. A eucharistic life is a life of contemplation and transformation. To contemplate Christ is to be transformed in Christ, and as one is transformed in Christ so, too, one incarnates Jesus' own attention and service to others. It is, in the language of Clare, following the footprints of Christ and becoming a mirror of Christ in one's life for others to see and follow.

Clare believed that a deep, loving relationship with the God of self-giving love leads us not only to union but to embodying that love in our own lives. In this respect, her "mysticism of motherhood" is intertwined with her eucharistic spirituality. Her language of motherhood underscores a deep, penetrating relationship of love with the crucified Spouse. It is a union of love that conceives the Word, carries the Word, gives birth to the Word and then is mirrored in the Word. Because this "motherhood" is none other than the imitation of Christ, it becomes a real image of Christ in the life of the believer when the soul can cry out of the Word delivered: "This is my Body." Her spirituality impels us to admit that we become what we conceive within us in the same way that we become what we love. Her spiritual path calls for active love, and only one who has entered into union with the crucified Spouse can become like the Spouse, crucified in love.

Transformation in Christ is central to a eucharistic life for Clare, and the renewal of Christ in one's life is the basis of the church which is the Body of Christ. In Clare's view, the Body of Christ grows when its members are active lovers, not passive listeners. Church membership is not an *affiliation* but a *participation* in the life of Christ. Those who are strengthened by grace must help the weaker members of the body so that it may grow towards its fullness in God. Clare indicates that only one who is on the path to God, who contemplates God and is transformed in God is truly a member of the church. Indeed, if one views her spiritual path from poverty to transformation one would have to say that the church is built on poverty, humility and love. When we fail in poverty, we fail in love, and when we fail in love the Body of Christ is weakened, the church is diminished. The return to poverty is at the heart of church renewal because it is a return to a eucharistic life, to the Eucharist *as* life and sacrament of God's presence in the world. Although Clare did not use the language of Eucharist or sacrament in her writings, her spirituality is centered on the idea that when the Body of Christ becomes the body of the believer, the body of the believer becomes the life of the church.

Living in the Body of Christ means renewing the gospel in the bodies of all those who follow Christ. In his book *Swimming in the Sun* Albert Haase writes, "We are the Body of Christ on earth. And every day, in some way, shape, or form, we are challenged to become the bread that is broken for the hungry of the world."[18] Eucharist is being bread broken and eaten for a hungry world. It is the food that gives the strength to make every stranger beloved. It is the "yes" of our lives to God's mysterious cruciform love. Yet, we must not forget its public nature. The Eucharist is like sharing a meal with a large family in a crowded restaurant. It requires attentiveness to others, patience, listening, sharing and forgiving the brother or sister who has taken the last bit of food. Miroslav Volf writes:

> We would most profoundly misunderstand the Eucharist...if we thought of it only as a sacrament of God's embrace of which we are simply the fortunate beneficiaries. Inscribed on the very heart of God's grace is the rule that we can be its recipients only if we do not resist being made into its agents; what happens to us must be done by us.[19]

Volf draws a connection between the Eucharist and the cross. In his book *Exclusion and Embrace* he states that the open arms of the crucified Christ signify a space in God's self for the other and an invitation for the enemy to come in.[20] The cross is not merely Christ's passion, Volf writes, but it is God's passion. It reveals the total self-giving love of God that reaches out to estranged humanity and embraces every stranger as the beloved.[21] In the cross we are embraced by the Trinity of love who loves us with the same love with which the persons of the Trinity love each other. In the cross, therefore, we are taken up in the eternal embrace of the triune God of love.[22] This embrace in love by the crucified Christ in which the arms of Christ are the arms of the triune God is, according to Volf, the meaning of Eucharist. "The eucharist," he writes, "is the ritual time in which we celebrate this divine making-space-for-us-and-inviting-us-in. However, it is not simply a being embraced by God but an empowering of God's love by which we are to embrace others, including our enemies. That is, "Having been embraced by God, we must make space for others in ourselves and invite them in—even our enemies."[23]

Understanding the Eucharist as the internalization of God's love leads to the centrality of the Eucharist as the basis of Catholic life. The truly catholic personality according to Orthodox theologian John Zizioulas is one centered around the mystery of the Eucharist. In receiving the Eucharist each person receives the whole Christ—head and members—so that the entire body is present in each member.[24] In this way, each person who partakes of the Eucharist is made into an ecclesial person and all persons are internal to the very being of each other. The Eucharist therefore signifies that each member is not external to the other members but rather internally related to the other members of the Body of Christ. Our relationship to Christ is our relationship to one another. If we say "yes" to the embrace of the crucified Christ then we must be willing to offer that embrace to our neighbor, our brother or sister, whoever he or she might be. For the person we willingly embrace has already been embraced by Christ.

As a mutual indwelling in the Body of Christ, Eucharist means celebrating the gift of self given to the other and the receiving of the other into the self.[25] But this giving and receiving entails suffering. Clare describes this image of suffering in the mirror of the cross. We are to gaze and contemplate this image of suffering humanity reflected in the crucified Christ: "All you who pass by the way, / look and see if there is any suffering / like my suffering!"[26] But she continues by indicating that as we see, so we are to love: "From this moment. .. let yourself be inflamed more strongly with the fervor of charity."[27] It is not enough to see suffering, we must unite with what we see by way of love. This is the meaning of the Eucharist because the Spirit of love that unites separate bodies in a unity of love is the Spirit that flows from the wounded side of Christ. If Eucharist means being embraced by God and embracing the other in God, then such embrace will bear the marks of the wounded Christ. This does mean necessarily that participation in the Eucharist will lead to the wounds of Christ; however, it does mean acceptance of weak, fragile humanity. It means we are willing to put aside our boundaries of dislike, anger, hurt, jealousy and whatever else may separate us and reach out in love. We may not want to live with a certain person but in their own weak frail humanity (as in ours) we see the reflection of God's goodness.

What made the lives of Francis and Clare so meaningful was not the idea that they were devoted followers of Christ (which they were) but rather that they allowed themselves to be embraced by the crucified

God and were willing to bear the wounds of reconciling love in their own bodies. As Volf states, "[W]e who have been embraced by the outstretched arms of the crucified God [must] open our arms even for the enemies—to make space in ourselves for them and invite them in—so that together we may rejoice in the eternal embrace of the triune God."[28] Francis, marked with the wounds of Christ, became an *alter Christus* (another Christ) because he continued to love his brothers to the end, including those who rejected him. Celano writes:

> [H]e grieved over those who now sank to the level of what was low and cheap, although they once had striven for higher things with all their desire.... So he prayed for God's mercy to set his sons free and fervently begged that they be preserved in the *grace given to them*.[29]

If Eucharist means finding ourselves internally related to every other person, including our enemies, and embracing the other in love, then it is indeed the source of a truly catholic personality and the seed of a new creation, whereby all humanity is bound in a unity of love. It is no wonder that Francis' biographers described him as the *vir catholicus*, the truly catholic man who, as Bonaventure wrote, symbolically returned to the state of original innocence through reconciliation with each and every thing.[30] Francis, living in the Body of Christ, became the body of Christ through the mystery of suffering and love. Embraced by God's compassionate love in the San Damiano cross, Francis strove to respond to that love by embracing the other, the leper or his enemy brother, and to receive that other within his own embrace of love through forgiveness and reconciliation.

The example of Francis as the eucharistic body of Christ speaks to us today in a world of violence and hatred. Whether it is enmity within our families or religious communities or the hatred that has spiraled in recent times among religions and nations, such enmity can only be overcome by a willingness to embrace the other in love. Albert Haase recounts the story of Corrie ten Boom who, with her family, was sent to the concentration camp at Ravensbruck for sheltering Jews. Only Corrie survived. After the war she committed herself to lecturing on the topic of forgiveness and reconciliation. Haase writes:

> One day after giving her talk in Munich, Germany, a man came forward to thank her for her talk. Corrie couldn't believe her eyes. He was one of the Nazi guards who used to stand duty in the women's shower room at Ravensbruck.
>
> The man reached out to shake Corrie's hand, but she froze. After all her talks on forgiveness, she could not reach out her hand in friendship. Her physical body remembered too sharply the horror of the camp and the death of her beloved sister. Corrie was blocked emotionally, stuck in the crippling and debilitating rut of resentment, bitterness, hatred.
>
> As Corrie stood there, frozen with shock, the battle raged inside of her. She was torn between the seductive desire to balance the scales of justice with violence and revenge and to heed Jesus' challenge of forgiveness which she herself had preached so often. So she prayed silently to herself, "Jesus, I cannot forgive this man. Give me your forgiveness."
>
> And as she prayed that prayer and as her mind's eye reviewed the years of brutality, suffering, humiliation, death, her hand suddenly lifted from her side! This former prisoner found herself offering the former shower guard the one thing she thought she did not know how to give. "I forgive you, brother, with all my heart!"[31]

The German theologian Dietrich Bonhoeffer once said that forgiveness is a form of suffering[32] because it means denying the desire for revenge. It is a type of suffering that Francis knew as he strove to forgive those who betrayed his ideals, that Corrie ten Boom knew as she faced her prison guard, and Bonhoeffer himself knew in the darkness of a concentration camp. But forgiveness is also the act of making a new future. It is giving an abundance of goodness so that a new future may be created and the past may be left behind. Beatrice Bruteau writes, "this 'intensified giving' which 'gives' itself 'away' is the heart of agape."[33] Each act of forgiveness is a new act of creation when we allow ourselves to let go so that the God of humble love may enter in. But the act of forgiveness must be nurtured by grace and strengthened by love because it requires a self-transcendence or, in the language of the Eucharist, to be broken and poured out so that others might have life. Francis challenged his followers to receive the Eucharist worthily because in this union with God we are mothers, sisters and brothers of Christ:

> All those...who receive the body and blood of our Lord Jesus Christ...are mothers when we carry Him in our heart and body through a divine love and a pure and sincere conscience and give birth to Him through a holy activity which must shine as an example before others.... O how holy and how loving...to have such a Brother and such as Son, our Lord Jesus Christ, Who laid down his life for his sheep."[34]

However he also indicated that it is better not to partake of the body and blood of Christ if we are unable to find ourselves internally related to one another and to embrace one another in love. He wrote: "let him eat and drink worthily because anyone who receives *unworthily, not distinguishing*, that is, not discerning, *the body of the Lord, eats and drinks judgment on himself*."[35] Although Clare left no writings on the Eucharist, her love of the sacrament was visible to those around her. The author of the "Versified Legend" captured the centrality of the Eucharist in Clare's life by saying "[t]he mind reveals itself by the fruit of its work, and its /outward deed manifests its intention / ... / as she sits, she spins cloth, cuts it into small palls / ... / a noble deed for adorning the altar and the Sacrament."[36] The author indicates that what we become in our lives is expressed outwardly in our deeds. Clare's life was an expression of the Eucharist, a life finely woven by the threads of love for the Crucified Spouse.

We see in the life of Francis and Clare that the Body of Christ is a flesh and blood reality. "Christ has no body now but yours," Teresa of Avila wrote, "no hands but yours, no feet but yours. Yours are the eyes through which must look out Christ's compassion on the world."[37] While Clare desires that we "[bring] Christ to life for the life of the world,"[38] she also calls us to participate in the life of the church. It is amazing that a woman living an enclosed life under ecclesiastical restrictions could express such an active participation in the church. Clare realized that when one is inflamed, like Christ crucified, with the fervor of charity, then one is willing to offer one's life for the sake of the gospel, and this self-offering is the food of life which nourishes the growth of the church.

Clare's spiritual path calls for active love and only one who has entered into union with the crucified Spouse can become like the Spouse, crucified in love. The church, in Clare's view, lives and grows when its members are active lovers not passive listeners. There is no greater joy or riches that money can buy nor can the church have any greater power than the living witness of Christ. For Clare, Christian life is the life of Christ and when that life is renewed through prayer and a deepening of love in union with God, the church becomes more fully the Body of Christ. This Body is life for the world and we are invited into this sacred banquet of life.

QUESTIONS FOR REFLECTION

1. How does the Eucharist shape your life? What role does it play in your view of the world?
2. How do you relate the Eucharist to inclusivity? How does the Eucharist help you live in the spirit of reconciliation and forgiveness?
3. How does the relationship between Eucharist and service influence community? Church? Ecumenical dialogue?
4. Does Clare's Christ mysticism pave the way for unity among world religions?
5. How is the whole universe becoming more Christic because of you?

NOTES

¹ Clare of Assisi, "The Third Letter to Agnes of Prague," 8 (Écrits, 102), Early Documents, p. 45.

² Clare of Assisi, "The Acts of the Process of Canonization," 9.2. Early Documents, p. 165.

³ According to the third witness of "The Acts of the Process of Canonization" (3.18), Clare declared to her sisters, "I want to be your hostage so that you do not do anything bad. If they come, place me before them." Early Documents, p. 150.

⁴ Clare of Assisi, "The Acts of the Process of Canonization," 6.6. Early Documents, p. 159.

⁵ Volf, Exclusion and Embrace, p. 47.

⁶ Volf, Exclusion and Embrace, p. 47

⁷ Volf, Exclusion and Embrace, p. 47.

⁸ "The Life of Saint Francis by Thomas of Celano," in FA:ED I, p. 263.

⁹ "The Life of Saint Francis by Thomas of Celano," in FA:ED I, p. 266.

¹⁰ Clare's ascetical practices were severe, at least according to the "Versified Legend of the Virgin Clare." The author writes that "she even lacerated her flesh with knots made from horse hair, / she made her bed on the bare ground, and sometimes broken/twigs were a bed, a couch is upon a slab of wood.... / Throughout the year, her food is bread, water her drink. / During the two Lents, she used to stop eating / on Mondays, Wednesdays and Fridays, / and took wine only on some Sundays." The practices were so severe, the author indicates, that Francis had to guide her to moderation of these practices. See "The Versified Legend of the Virgin Clare," XV, Early Documents, p. 203.

¹¹ "The Life of Saint Francis by Thomas of Celano," in FA:ED I, p. 266.

¹² "The Life of Saint Francis by Thomas of Celano," in FA:ED I, p. 267.

¹³ Clare of Assisi, "The Acts of the Process of Canonization," 2.1–3, Early Documents, pp. 141–142.

¹⁴ "The Life of Saint Francis by Thomas of Celano," 9.115 in FA:ED I, p. 283.

¹⁵ N. Max Wildiers, The Theologian and his Universe: Theology and Cosmology from the Middle Ages to the Present (New York: Seabury, 1982), p. 222.

¹⁶ "The Acts of the Process of Canonization," 3.9, Early Documents, p. 148.

¹⁷ Michael W. Blastic, "Clare of Assisi, The Eucharist and John 13," in Clare of Assisi: Investigations, F. Edward Coughlin, ed. (St. Bonaventure, N.Y.: The Franciscan Institute Press, 1993), pp. 36–37.

¹⁸ Albert Haase, Swimming in the Sun: Discovering the Lord's Prayer with Francis of Assisi and Thomas Merton (Cincinnati: St. Anthony Messenger Press, 1993), pp. 143–144.

¹⁹ Volf, Exclusion and Embrace, p. 129.

²⁰ Volf, Exclusion and Embrace, p. 126.

²¹ Volf, Exclusion and Embrace, p. 127.

²² Volf, Exclusion and Embrace, p. 129.

²³ Volf, Exclusion and Embrace, p. 129.

[24] John Zizioulas, *Being as Communion: Studies in Personhood and the Church* (Crestwood: St. Vladimir's Seminary Press, 1985), p. 58.

[25] Volf, *Exclusion and Embrace*, p. 130.

[26] Clare of Assisi, "The Fourth Letter to Agnes of Prague," 24–25 (*Écrits*, 114), *Early Documents*, p. 51.

[27] Clare of Assisi, "The Fourth Letter to Agnes of Prague," 27 (*Écrits*, 116), *Early Documents*, p. 51.

[28] Volf, *Exclusion and Embrace*, p. 131.

[29] "The Life of Saint Francis by Thomas of Celano," in *FA:ED I*, p. 274.

[30] Bonaventure *Legenda maior* 8.1 (EM, 64). Bonaventure writes: "True piety. . . drew him up to God through devotion, transformed him into Christ through compassion, attracted him to his neighbor through condescension and symbolically showed a return to the state of original innocence through universal reconciliation with each and every thing." *Bonaventure: The Soul's Journey Into God*, p. 250.

[31] Albert Haase, pp. 162–163.

[32] Dietrich Bonhoeffer, *The Cost of Discipleship*, R. H. Fuller, trans. (New York: Macmillan, 1963), p. 100.

[33] Beatrice Bruteau, *The Grand Option: Personal Transformation and a New Creation* (South Bend, Ind.: University of Notre Dame Press, 2001), p. 129.

[34] Francis of Assisi, "Earlier Exhortation to the Brothers and Sisters of Penance" (The First Version of the Letter to the Faithful), 1, 3, 10, 13 in *FA:ED I*, pp. 41–42.

[35] Francis of Assisi, "Later Admonition and Exhortation to the Brothers and Sisters of Penance" (Second Version of the Letter to the Faithful) 24 in *FA:ED I*, p. 47.

[36] "The Versified Legend of the Virgin Clare," XXIV, *Early Documents*, p. 211.

[37] This prayer is attributed to Saint Teresa of Avila.

[38] Brunelli, "Contemplation in the Following of Jesus Christ," p. 167.

Chapter Eight

THE POWER OF THE SPIRIT

The student of Franciscan spirituality comes to know rather quickly that relationship with God is centered in the person of Jesus Christ. We find this centrality in the writings of Francis of Assisi, in Bonaventure and, significantly, in Clare's writings. We have already traveled the path from the poverty of gazing to the height of transformation and, yet, there is more to be said. Clare's thought is like a cross-stitch pattern on fine cloth. It arises from a deep center of a heart full of grace. Just as the beauty of a sewn pattern emerges from the skilled hand of the seamstress, so too, the beauty of Christ emerges from the prayerful life of the believer. What enables the seamstress to create a beautiful pattern is the energy of attentiveness, focus and delicate handwork. What forms the Christ life of the believer is faith, attentiveness to the presence of God and the interior life of the Spirit. The seamstress, like the believer, demands an intensity of the Spirit because it is the Spirit who is the energy of life and who creates all things new. Clare is the skillful seamstress who allows the energies of the Spirit to thread through her own incarnational life.

Clare's spirituality, centered in Christ, is empowered by the Spirit. It is the Spirit that calls her into the mystery of Christ, and it is the Spirit that energizes her life as she plumbs the mystery. Francis said that to follow Christ one must be "inwardly cleansed, interiorly enlightened and *inflamed* [emphasis added] by the fire of the Holy Spirit."[1] He did not say "filled" with the Spirit but "inflamed" by the Spirit, as if the Spirit is a great bonfire in the midst of the soul propelling it toward God. Perhaps he saw this fire in the life of Clare who was drawn to the mountain of union with God by the fire of the Spirit who enkindled her life. Clare herself described the Spirit as the gravity of love that draws the believer toward God. In her view, the Spirit is like a magnet of love that can hardly be avoided unless we are so completely preoccupied with ourselves that we are oblivious to the fire of God's love within. The Spirit is the divine life-giving energy that draws the soul in a dynamic movement toward God, as she indicated in her second letter to Agnes: "[M]ay you go forward / securely, joyfully, and swiftly, / on the path of prudent happiness, / ... / in the pursuit of that perfection / to which the Spirit of the Lord has called you."[2]

The Spirit of the Lord is a rather elusive person of the Trinity. While it is easy to imagine the Father and form a relationship to the Son, it is more difficult to grasp the Holy Spirit. For the Spirit is just that—Spirit. Yet, the Holy Spirit is a person and, as person, integral to the shape of concrete reality. The Holy Spirit is personal because the Spirit is intimately associated with the persons of the Father and Son and is the bond of love between them, a bond not as in a handshake but as in a child whose birth could only come about through the love of one to another. Of course, Clare has no elaborate theology of the Spirit but she does express three aspects of the spiritual life that reflect the profound role of the Spirit in her life. These aspects are: joy, freedom and dynamic movement. All three aspects of the Spirit permeate her letters to Agnes.

In her fourth letter to Agnes, composed two years before Clare died, and probably from her sickbed, Clare speaks of "joy in the Spirit" as she wrote, "I rejoice and exult with you *in the joy of the Spirit* (1 Thes 1:6)." Had Clare not been inflamed by the Spirit which permeated her life she probably would have written something to the effect: "After all these years of fighting for the privilege of poverty and preserving the authenticity of our life through constant battle if not rebellion, I must say, I have had enough. I am ready to go home to God." But Clare utters nothing like this. She writes her final letter to Agnes as if in the youth of her spiritual life. She is filled with hope, love and desire, as if she has just discovered the source of happiness, the pearl of great price. She writes:

Happy, indeed, is she
   to whom it is given to share in this sacred banquet
   so that she might cling with all her heart
   to Him
      Whose beauty all the blessed hosts of heaven unceasingly
         admire,
      Whose affection excites
      Whose contemplation refreshes,
      Whose kindness fulfills,
      Whose delight replenishes,
      Whose remembrance delightfully shines,
      By Whose fragrance the dead are revived,
      Whose glorious vision will bless
      all the citizens of the heavenly Jerusalem:
      which, *since it is the splendor of eternal glory,* is
         the brilliance of eternal light
         and the mirror without blemish.[3]

From where does this youthful spirit of joy arise? From the most unlikely source which is key to Clare's spirituality, the *"mirror without blemish,"* that is, the mirror of the cross. It is the mature, deep, contemplative gaze on the crucified Christ, a lifetime of gazing, that generates in Clare the Spirit of confidence in the love of God and the spiritual transformation of her own life into the image of Christ. In the midst of her physical afflictions and the difficulties of community life, Clare found a wellspring of joy in the Spirit, a joy that arose from accepting the poverty of her humanity, from self-identity, from living a virtuous life, and from a heart full of love that could see and respond to the suffering of another. But Clare's joy also arose out of freedom. The poverty of the cross and the outpouring of God's love utterly convinced her of the promise of heaven, as she first wrote to Agnes: "O holy poverty, / God promises the kingdom of heaven / and, in fact, offers eternal glory and a blessed life / to those who possess and desire you!"[4] Her decision to follow Francis' way of life from the outset was a free decision to follow the poor Crucified. There is little doubt that Clare had an inner

strength that impelled her to keep going in the face of immense difficulties and obstacles. This inner strength, I believe, arose from her spiritual grasp of God's overflowing love for her shown in the cross. She
was undeterred by the implications of the cross—suffering and death—
and, instead, opted to live the paradoxical life of the cross because she
was convinced of the promise of eternal life. "[If you] die with Him on
the cross of tribulation, / you shall possess heavenly mansions *in the
splendor of the saints*," she wrote to Agnes.[5] Clare indicates that if we are
free to die we are free to live because we are free for God. Only the
poor person can be truly free, that is free for God, because the poor
person clings to God and to nothing else other than God. This freedom
to live in the paradox of the cross was a source of joy for Clare because
it was a deepening of life in God, forming the inextricable bonds of
love that would bound her forever in the eternal embrace of the Trinity.

Clare shows a real sense of moving forward into God. Her language is dynamic and directional. She does not waver in her letters to
Agnes but instead shows determinism and confidence in God's love and
the promise of eternal life. She lives in hope nurtured by faith by which
she has an assurance of things yet unseen. In her second letter to Agnes
she tells her to "go forward / securely, joyfully, and swiftly, / on the path
of prudent happiness, / not believing anything / not agreeing with anything / that would dissuade you from this resolution."[6] Go forward into
God. How often do we turn back because we lose confidence or are
deterred by failure? Jesus himself said, "No one who puts a hand to the
plow and looks back is fit for the kingdom of God" (Luke 9:62). Jesus,
like Clare, wants us to go forward in the direction of God's reign. But
what impels us to go forward into God when everything seems to fail
or fall apart around us? Clare's answer, I believe, is the power of the
Spirit, not the elusive "Holy Ghost" but the Spirit of concrete reality,
the Spirit of crucified love. It is the Spirit, she indicates, who draws us,
pulls us and empowers us to aim our lives toward the heart of the
Trinity, even when we are living in the midst of the cross. Go forward,
swiftly and securely into God, she wrote to Agnes, at a time when the
welfare of her community was being challenged by the church

hierarchy. There is no doubt that Clare was motivated by the love of God and she would settle for nothing less than the full experience of that love. Even at the end of her life when she was sick and frail, her spirit showed the lightness of a youth in love, as she proclaimed: "I will run and not tire, / until You *bring me into the wine-cellar*, / until Your *left hand is under my head* / and Your *right hand will embrace me* happily, / [and] *You will kiss me with the* happiest *kiss of your mouth*."[7]

One senses that, for Clare, life in God was a perpetual deepening of union in love, a constant progression "from good to better, from virtue to virtue."[8] Her spirituality of love bears a likeness to the fourth-century writer Gregory of Nyssa and his doctrine of *epektasis*.[9] According to Gregory, the soul continually longs for God and continually reaches out for him. However, there is no ultimate satisfaction, no final union, no ecstasy in which the soul achieves union. Rather, *epektasis* describes the perpetual growth of the soul ("tension" or "expansion"). It expresses the soul's constant motion forward as it forgets what is past and continually opens to new graces. The soul is conceived as a spiritual universe in eternal expansion towards the infinite source of love. The soul of the human person, like Clare, continues to expand in love which knows no boundaries. On one hand there is a certain contact with God, a real participation and divinization. The soul is, in a true sense, transformed into the divine; it truly participates in the Spirit. But God who is *infinite* love remains constantly beyond, and the soul must always go out of itself, that is, it must continually go beyond the stage it has reached to make a further discovery. Thus each stage is a "glory" but the brilliance of each stage is always being obscured by the new "glory"; thus the soul moves from glory to glory (see 2 Corinthians 3:18). Because change is the mark of spiritual growth, sin is the ultimate refusal to grow. For Gregory, the soul's security is in change. If or when the soul stops growing and changing, it falls away from stability. While the soul's desire is at each moment fulfilled by participation in God and thus attains some perfection, such participation expands the soul further and makes it capable of a still higher degree of participation. Thus each new stage of spiritual growth is the development of a reality that is entirely new. The journey into God is like a spiral. Every stage of growth in the soul is an absolute beginning or, we might say, every ending is a beginning, and every arrival is a new departure.

Although Clare does not speak the theological language of Gregory, still her movement toward God connotes a type of perpetual ascent, being drawn by the infinite love of God toward happiness, fulfillment and immense joy. There is light and levity in her pursuit of holiness, as if each discovery of God's immense love is a new beginning. She tells Agnes to go forward into God "with swift pace, light step / unswerving feet, / so that even your steps stir up no dust."[10] One gets the impression that if Clare had wings, she would fly into God. While her language is light and airy, it also suggests that the things of the world are not to weigh us down, that God is always the core of our limited existence, which is weak and fragile. Even at the end of her life, she speaks of running into the embrace of God: "I will run and not tire," she says. She is not only filled with the Spirit but she is drawn by the Spirit of love in an ever-deepening way, the way of union with the crucified (and glorified) Christ. For the joy she speaks of is inextricably linked with the mirror of the Crucified. Herein is one of the underlying mysteries of Clare's spirituality, empowerment by the Spirit through the cross of Christ. Whereas suffering can weigh us down and death seems like the final end, Clare sees hope in the midst of the cross, that is, she looks toward the divine promises.

The author of the Letter to the Hebrews writes: "Now faith is the assurance of things hoped for, the conviction of things not seen" (Hebrews 11:1). Clare has a conviction of things not seen. She could easily have been thwarted in her pursuit of God by the many difficulties she encountered but her spiritual directives indicate otherwise. She knows in the deepest center of her life that human nature is weak and sin is a reality, that God has entered into the weakness of our humanity and that God's generosity cannot be outdone. Clare sees the cross not as a sign of failure but as a sign of glory. She is convinced that what we suffer in this life can never outweigh the glory that awaits us. As she contemplates her life in the mystery of the cross, she is strengthened by the Spirit of crucified love. She tells Agnes, therefore, to gaze daily on the mirror of the cross so that she will attain not only transformation in Christ but joy in the Spirit, for it is the Spirit who leads us into the uncharted depths of God's love.

It is likely that one could weave a whole Trinitarian design through Clare's textured spirituality, for she begins with the God of outpouring love in the cross and ends with joy in the Spirit, centering her thought on the poor crucified Spouse. But she also integrates the pattern of the believer's life in this Trinitarian design. The faithful soul is not an innocent bystander to the profound mystery of the Incarnation but participates in the life of this mystery. In Bonaventure's view, we are created to the image of Christ because our salvation is necessary for the completion of Christ or, as Clare wrote to Agnes, "I consider you a *co-worker of God* Himself (cf. 1 Cor 3:9; Rm 16:3) and a support of the weak members of His ineffable Body."[11] What the saints grasp is that the way we live our lives in God makes a profound difference—we either help build up the Body of Christ or we diminish it. In Clare's view (as well as Bonaventure's) we help build up the Body of Christ by putting on Christ in our own lives so that we can say "it is no longer I who live, but it is Christ who lives in me" (Galatians 2:20). To "put on Christ" is a difficult idea to grasp but it is the essence of Christian life. In his spiritual writings, Bonaventure indicates that unless we put on Christ, the mystery we name as "Christ" is incomplete, because the completion of Christ depends on us. Clare contributes to this idea in her own way. She considers Agnes a "co-worker" of God, one who can help support the weak members of Christ's Body and help build up this Body in love. We may think this requires special action or involvement in the church and world. But Clare wrote from with the enclosure of her convent. I believe that it was precisely the geography of her spiritual life that enabled her to ponder the Christ mystery through the lens of the human person. Whereas Francis and Bonaventure emphasized the universality of Christ, Clare points to the *particularity* of the Christ mystery. What she indicates is that our own unique personhood as image of God is fulfilled in Christ, and the mystery of Christ, which includes the meaning of the universe, is fulfilled in our humanity. In a sense, Jesus

Christ, in his risen and eternal life, is what we are called to be in this earthly, finite life, that is, the praise and glory of the Father. The life of Jesus Christ is the pattern of unifying love not only for our own lives but for the whole creation.

This relationship between the believer and Christ is an awesome and tremendous mystery. Raimon Panikkar states that "God is mystery and we too exist within this mystery."[12] We are caught up in the "I-Thou" relationship of the Father and Son in such a way that, like Jesus, we, too, are the "you" of the Father.[13] Although we are not the Son of God, we are little words of the Word of God, finite expressions of the infinite love of the Father expressed in the Son. We, too, therefore are entwined in the infinite "Thou-ing" of the Father. That we are caught up in the awesome mystery of the Trinity is difficult to comprehend. It is much easier to imagine God as an elderly grandfather, the Son as our brother, and the Spirit as something that wistfully surrounds us. But the fact is, our lives are involved in the mystery of Christ who is the center of the Trinity and the center of creation. Christ is the firstborn of creation, the meaning of the cosmos, the first in God's intention to love. Without our participation in the Christ mystery, creation lacks meaning and purpose, and God's desire to love is thwarted. Indeed, without creation and humankind, Christ does not exist because Christ is the Word Incarnate, and the incarnation of that Word is fulfilled in us, and through us, in creation itself. Although Clare does not expound this idea, she is no exception to the Franciscan emphasis on the primacy of Christ.[14] Her incarnational spirituality centered on the crucified Christ focuses on love and transformation, not sin and guilt. She clearly follows the idea that Christ is first in God's intention to love. Christ is the meaning of the cosmos, as she wrote to Agnes, "may you totally love Him / ... / Whose beauty the sun and the moon admire."[15] We are to be transformed in Christ because we are to be transformed in love, and love is the meaning and purpose of the cosmos. The Incarnation is not the end of human longing but the beginning of what we and all creation have been called into from eternity, the fullness of Christ. The emergence of God in fragile humanity signifies a powerful explosion in history, an explosion we can liken today to the big bang, from which our universe story began almost fourteen billion years ago.

How does the fullness of Christ come to be realized in creation? Panikkar suggests that it is through the power of the Spirit. It is the Spirit sent by Christ that enkindles the Christ mystery within us and among us. It is significant that Christ does not impart the Spirit during his earthly life but the Spirit is sent upon his death and resurrection. "Unless I go away," Jesus said, "the Paraclete will not come to you; but if I go, I will send him to you" (see John 16:7). In the Gospel of John we realize that Jesus must go away in order for the Spirit to come. The departure of Jesus is the arrival of the Spirit. The going away of the earthly Jesus is the beginning of the resurrected Christ made possible by the Spirit. One must wonder why Jesus could not stay to finish the work he had begun. Instead, he promises the Spirit to his followers at a moment when his whole mission borders on the brink of disaster. Panikkar writes:

> [T]he future does not seem bright, his followers will be persecuted... [T]he Master is about to leave them...without having finished hardly anything while, at the same time, almost abandoning them....
>
> The people have abandoned him because it has become too risky to follow him; the synagogue declares him a heretic, indeed blasphemous; the political representatives despise him; and his "own" do not understand him. He has not left them anything durable, no institution; he has neither baptized nor ordained, much less has he founded anything.... He has left both the Spirit and himself as a silent Presence in the eucharistic act. He has sent [his disciples] as lambs among wolves and refuses to change tactics even at the end: wolves are still roaming about. He promises his followers only one thing: the Spirit.[16]

There is something worth noting about Jesus' imminent departure at a time when his mission was just getting underway and his disciples were gaining in number. Jesus does not stay around to complete his earthly work; rather, he promises the Spirit to his disciples for it is they, he indicates, who will complete his work. Imagine the utter amazement and confusion of the disciples during the final days of Jesus' earthly life. How could they perform greater works than Jesus? Indeed, they feared the loss of their Master and teacher. But the answer is simply the power of the Spirit. Through the power of the Spirit, Jesus indicated that his disciples could do greater works than him, for the Spirit does new things, and only in the Spirit can this world move forward toward the fullness of life in God. Thus, Jesus said to his disciples, "It is good that I am leaving you." "Otherwise," Panikkar writes, "we would make him king—that is, an idol—or we would rigidify him into concepts, into intellectual containers. We would turn his teaching into a system, imprison him within our own categories and suffocate the Spirit."[17] Rather, Jesus knew that it was good that he leave, that he had not come to remain but to remain in us in the most perfect form, not as a more or less welcome guest foreign to us but in our very being. This is the meaning of the Eucharist. This is the work of the Spirit and the meaning of Christ: "I am with you always, to the end of the age" (Matthew 28:20). Jesus leaves so that the dynamism of life will not be reduced to an arid dualism. His departure does not signify the departure of God from the world but the release of God into the world. This release of God is the power of the Spirit who infiltrates our lives in the name of Christ and reconstitutes the Body of Christ in a new way, the way of unifying love amidst the delightful diversity of God's creation.

It is this release of God into the world that helps us impart a deeper meaning to Clare's spirituality. Again, while her spirituality is thoroughly incarnational it is enlivened by the Spirit who permeates the path to transformation in Christ. The Spirit draws us into the embrace of God's love, as she writes in her fourth letter to Agnes: *"Draw me after you, / we will run in the fragrance of your perfumes."*[18] The "you" of this passage is the beloved Spouse who, for Clare, is the crucified Christ. We are drawn to the beloved by the fragrance of the Crucified Christ's life. Gazing on the mirror of the Crucified and risen Christ refreshes, fulfills and replenishes the life of the believer, because by the fragrance of the Crucified, the dead are brought to life.[19] What is this fragrance that

Clare speaks about? A fragrance is usually associated with perfume, a sweet-smelling liquid that when applied, diffuses its delightful odor that can attract others. The fragrance is not the perfume itself (that is the liquid) but the odor which the perfume diffuses. Thus we are drawn to the perfume (or repelled by it!) according to the odor that emanates from it. The Spirit is like the fragrance of love that diffuses from the life of Christ. It is that odor of love that is left behind after the departure of Jesus from earthly life. Was this "odor" of the Spirit not already present in the life of Jesus? Yes, but the fullness of the Spirit's presence could not be comprehended because the earthly life of Jesus was limited by its "earthiness," that is, confusion, misunderstanding, rejection and the limitations of his life did not allow the disciples to fully grasp the meaning of Jesus' life. Thus, Jesus had to die in order for the fullness of the Spirit to come and the fullness of God to be revealed. It is only *after* the death of Jesus that the church is born because it is born from the power of the Spirit who opened the hearts of the disciples, and those that followed, to the meaning of Jesus' life.

Clare writes of being revived, brought to life, by the fragrance of the beloved crucified Spouse. She desires to run in the fragrance of his perfumes. Because fragrance elicits desire, one can only surmise that her desire to be drawn into union with the beloved was made possible by the fragrance of crucified love. This fragrance of love is the power of the Spirit. It is so strong that we are drawn to it, we run after it, and thus we are drawn into the mystery of Christ. The same Spirit that draws us into the mystery of Christ transforms us in Christ; the Spirit of attraction is the Spirit of transformation. We become "another Christ" through the power of the Spirit. Both Celano and Bonaventure grasped this relationship between the Spirit and Christ as they reflected on the life of Francis. What made Francis "another Christ" according to Bonaventure, was not literal imitation of Christ but the excess of love which bore itself out in Francis' willingness to suffer like Christ. Francis was "transformed in the likeness of Christ crucified not by martyrdom of his flesh," Bonaventure said, "but by the enkindling of his soul." His encounter with the crucified Christ in the form of a seraph on the mount of La Verna left in his heart a "marvelous fire." In his "Major Legend of Saint Francis" Bonaventure wrote:

After true love of Christ
transformed the lover *into his image,* .

...

the angelic man Francis
came down from the mountain,
bearing with him
the likeness of the Crucified,

...

engraved on parts of his flesh
by the finger of the living God.[20]

And what is the "finger of the living God?" It is the Holy Spirit, as Bonaventure tells us in his *Hexaëmeron*: "Because this wisdom is attained only through grace, all hidden and unforeseeable things [are attributed] to the Holy Spirit.... *This is the finger of God.*"[21] This power of love that transformed Francis, therefore, was the Spirit for it is the Spirit sent by Christ who conforms us to Christ. The Spirit sets us free because the Spirit leads us to the truth of who we are in God. Francis was truly a free man because he lived in the power of the Spirit, and in this power of love he became the new life of Christ in the world. Jesus risen from the dead was alive in Francis. Through the power of love he became a new image of Christ, an *alter Christus*, for others to see and follow.

We would be remiss, however, to think that Francis had a carefree life of holiness. Like Jesus, Francis was misunderstood and rejected even by his own brothers. According to Grado Merlo, the acceptance of clerics and theologians into the order changed the shape and original intuition of Francis. By the time the *Earlier Rule* was composed, Francis resigned from government of the order and began to distance himself from it due to deep conflicts with the theologians and lawyers who had entered and were forging a different path, contrary to his desires.[22] His sojourn on the mount of La Verna was a long period of resentful solitude, painfully dissatisfied at how the consequences of his "inspired" way of life were being expressed in the life of the order.[23] It is in light of *this* experience of suffering that Francis received the stigmata, perhaps facing the decisive and supreme sacrifice of his will by accepting and sharing in the great sufferings of Christ through his personal "passion."[24] Francis descended the mountain filled with peace, yet a peace which included suffering, the peace which follows the path of the crucified Christ. Descending the mountain of La Verna with the wounds of Christ engraved in his flesh, Francis began to take up again his ministry to the lepers, committed to his original inspiration of minority and fraternity despite the new obstacles of the order.

What we see in the life of Francis, as in the life of Clare, is a commitment to love despite the wounds and failures of earthly life. Even in the depths of his cross, Francis remained faithful to God and resolved to live the compassionate love that first touched his heart, that is, he remained faithful in love unto death. The greatness of Francis was probably less appreciated in his lifetime than after his death; the first biography was written in 1228, two years after he died. Like Jesus, Francis had to depart this world in order for the power of his spirit to come into it and take root in the hearts of his disciples. What we see in the life of Francis, as in the life of Jesus, is the transcendent nature of the Spirit. Although the Spirit works in our lives to conform us in love to God, the fullness of who we are in God can only be fully revealed after our death, when the boundaries of our lives no longer pose an obstacle to the work of God in us. How we live in relation to God in our earthly lives, therefore, makes a difference in what type of spirit we impart to the world. Once death shatters our finite earthly vessels of human clay, then the spiritual fragrance of our lives is released into the world. Another way of saying this is, the way we journey to God influences the type of spirit we leave behind, a spirit that can either attract or repel others to Christ. The spirit of our lives can either help others go to God or it may fail to generate new life.

The forward movement into God that Clare describes is a movement that begins in this life and endures unto eternal life. However, it is also leaving behind the fragrance of the Spirit that shapes our lives.

Death is not the final end of our existence but rather the opening up of our full personalities in the universe. What we impart to the world upon our deaths is not our writings or books or worldly treasures but the spiritual fragrance of our lives. What will that fragrance be? Will it be the fragrance of holiness that inspires others to run after God? Or will it be a pungent fragrance that causes others to abandon the Christ mystery? Although the saints are seldom recognized as saints in their lifetimes, what makes them stand apart after their deaths is the fragrance of love they leave behind. We see in their lives the deeper meaning of the Christ mystery. They bring to life the mission of Jesus, especially in his death and resurrection. We recognize in the saints that Jesus departs from this world to become something more for the world—the Christ—the beloved Word and Wisdom of the Father. The Spirit is what brings Christ to the fullness of life in creation: "If I do not go away," Jesus said, "the Advocate will not come to you; but if I go, I will send him to you. And when he comes.... He will glorify me" (John 16:7–8, 14). Jesus departs from the world to become the fullness of life for the world, the fullness of what he has been from eternity, the beloved of the Father. What God had intended for all eternity—the Christ—now becomes concrete reality in the person of Jesus who in his death and resurrection is anointed as the Christ—the Incarnate Word risen and glorified. Because the humanity of Jesus is our humanity, what happens in Jesus is our destination as well—transformation and union in God. The saints are those who enter into this Christ mystery by their wholehearted commitment to Christ, not simply in their earthly lives but more so in their eternal lives. The intense, fragrant spirit of love they leave behind becomes a powerful force of holiness in the world that draws others to Christ and helps build up the Body of Christ on earth.

That is why it is essential how the Spirit takes root in our lives because we, too, are called to be saints. The spiritual life is not simply about our personal transformation in God; rather, the transforming power of the Spirit in our lives influences how we help build up the Body of Christ—the reign of God here on earth. Jesus indicated by his radical departure from earthly life and the sending of the Spirit, that the whole creation has yet to become the fullness of Christ. He said to his disciples, "As the Father has loved me, so I have loved you; abide in my love" (John 15:9). We are asked to *continue* the Incarnation, to allow the Word of God to take root within us, to allow it to become enfleshed in us. The Incarnation is not finished; it is not yet fully complete for it is to be complete in us. As Panikkar states, continuation of the Incarnation "liberates us from living in a merely historical and temporal universe and makes us conscious of our divine dignity."[25] We are called to continue that Incarnation toward the new Incarnation, the fullness of Christ, which is all humanity and creation bound in a union of love.

It is likely that a Spirit Christology would have been beyond the scope of Clare's vision and, yet, her insights woven in her spiritual directives to a woman she never met, points to the profound implications of the Christ mystery. Her language of image, transformation, fragrance, perfumes and running toward God leads us to suggest that living in the Incarnation is a dynamic relationship of love. What we become in our relationship to Christ shapes our future in God, and what we become in relation to God influences what we leave behind in death, as we impart the spirit of our lives to the evolution of the new creation in Christ. Life in God is more than a temporal, feel-good, comforting experience. Rather, how we go forth into God influences the spiritual energy of love we bequeath to the world. As we receive the Spirit sent by Christ, so too, Christ is born within us. As Christ is born within us, so too, our "spiritual personalities" begin to permeate the universe. Salvation becomes more than us and Jesus; rather, it becomes our unique participation in the Christ mystery. Just as Jesus promised the Spirit to his disciples before he died, so too, do we participate in this mission. As death shatters the vessels of our earthly bodies, our spirits are released into the universe to help shape it anew in Christ through the power of memory and presence. We are coworkers with God, helping to build up the Body of Christ, not only in our earthly lives but even more so in eternal life. Our forward movement into God through faith, hope and love is a "leaving behind," a bequeathing of our christified spirits to the world so that others may be drawn into the mystery of Christ.

What Clare's spirituality helps us realize is that, while our individual lives may seem insignificant in view of the immensity of the universe, each of us has a unique part to play in the unfolding of God's mystery in creation. It is the Spirit, the weaver of life in creation, who takes the threads of our lives and weaves them into a quilt of many colors that clothes the Body of Christ in the universe. The work of the Spirit clothing the Body of Christ in creation is a movement of love. Clare reminds us that we are on a journey in love but we are not alone. We join with all the saints who have gone before us, are with us and will come after us. Clare is among them and she is with us as sister, mother and guide.

QUESTIONS FOR REFLECTION

1. How do you understand the relationship between the Spirit and Christ?
2. How did Clare live her relationship to Christ by following the Spirit? How do you?
3. Do you live in a "forward movement" or a "backward movement"? Do you live in the past and strive for the future? What is the role of the Spirit in the movement of your life?
4. Do you live in the promise of God? With trust? Faith? Hope? Conviction? Do you believe that the cross leads us to the victory of love? How does the Spirit help you participate in this victory of love?
5. What is your life's fragrance?

NOTES

1 Francis of Assisi, "A Letter to the Entire Order" 51 in *FA:ED I*, p. 120.
2 Clare of Assisi, "The Second Letter to Agnes of Prague," 13–14 (*Écrits*, 94), *Early Documents*, p. 41.
3 Clare of Assisi, "The Fourth Letter to Agnes of Prague," 9–14 (*Écrits*, 112), *Early Documents*, p. 50.
4 Clare of Assisi, "The First Letter to Agnes of Prague," 16 (*Écrits*, 86), *Early Documents*, p. 36.
5 Clare of Assisi, "The Second Letter to Agnes of Prague," 21 (*Écrits*, 98), *Early Documents*, p. 42.
6 Clare of Assisi, "The Second Letter to Agnes of Prague," 13–14 (*Écrits*, 94), *Early Documents*, p. 41.
7 Clare of Assisi, "The Fourth Letter to Agnes of Prague," 31–32 (*Écrits*, 116), *Early Documents*, p. 52.
8 Clare of Assisi, "The First Letter to Agnes of Prague," 32 (*Écrits*, 90), *Early Documents*, p. 38.
9 For a discussion of *epektasis* see Andrew Louth, "Gregory of Nyssa" in *Origins of the Christian Mystical Tradition: From Plato to Denys* (New York: Oxford, 1981), pp. 89–90.
10 Clare of Assisi, "The Second Letter to Agnes of Prague," 12 (*Écrits*, 94), *Early Documents*, p. 41.
11 Clare of Assisi, "The Third Letter to Agnes of Prague," 8 (*Écrits*, 102), *Early Documents*, p. 45.
12 Raimon Panikkar, *Christophany: The Fullness of Man* (Maryknoll, N.Y.: Orbis, 2004), p. 106.
13 Panikkar, *Christophany*, p. xvi.
14 The "primacy of Christ," described most clearly by Duns Scotus, says that the Incarnation is not due to sin but to the love of God. Christ is first in God's intention to love. For a discussion on the primacy of Christ see Ilia Delio, "Revisiting the Franciscan Doctrine of Christ," *Theological Studies* 64.1 (March 2003), pp. 3–23.
15 Clare of Assisi, "The Third Letter to Agnes of Prague," 16 (*Écrits*, 104), *Early Documents*, p. 46.
16 Panikkar, *Christophany*, p. 122.
17 Panikkar, *Christophany*, p. 124.
18 Clare of Assisi, "The Fourth Letter to Agnes of Prague," 30 (*Écrits*, 116), *Early Documents*, 51.
19 Clare of Assisi, "The Fourth Letter to Agnes of Prague," 11–13 (*Écrits*, 112), *Early Documents*, p. 50.
20 Bonaventure, "The Major Legend of Saint Francis" 13.5 in *FA:ED II*, p. 634.
21 Bonaventure, *Hex.* 2.30 (VIII, p. 341).
22 Grado Giovanni Merlo, "The Story of Brother Francis and the Order of Friars Minor," Edward Hagman, trans. *Greyfriars Review* 15.1 (2001), p. 7.
23 Merlo, "Story of Brother Francis," p. 9.
24 Merlo, "Story of Brother Francis," p. 9.
25 Panikkar, *Christophany*, p. 128.

Conclusion

Every person, from childhood on, is asked at least once, "What do you want to be when you grow up?" Usually we want to be something glamorous or noble or valiant. Rarely does someone answer, "I want to be myself." Yet that is what Clare hopes for Agnes, that she will become herself because in that self God lives, and where God lives, God acts, and where God acts God is made visible to the world. Clare's letters come across as seemingly simple. But they are actually dense with meaning and so profound. They bear the fruit of deep reflection on the tremendous and awesome love of God. Because Clare is so convinced of God's abiding presence in the Incarnation, she shows little fear and much confidence in the power of God's love. This is the love, she says, that can raise the dead to life and can transform our ordinary, humdrum lives into the living presence of Christ. Transformation is at the heart of Clare's spirituality because when the power of God's love takes hold of the life of the believer, Christ is born anew.

The gravity of love for Clare that draws us into God is the love of the crucified Christ. Clare speaks about running into the arms of crucified love, as if the cross is made of flowers and garlands rather than wood and nails. Her spirituality is disarming because when we think of the cross, we think of sin, guilt, expiation and justification. Rarely do we think about love. Yet Clare sees the cross neither as a sign of guilt nor the consequence of sin (although she is clearly aware of sin). Rather she sees the poverty of the crucified Christ reflecting the poverty of God, who is love. Poverty and love co-inhere in Clare's thought. Just as God gives everything to us in love, so too we must be free and unhindered to accept that love and in turn share that love with others. While such an idea may warm the heart, Clare's affective spirituality is demanding. It is not simply that God loves us but God loves us by entering into weak, fragile human flesh and suffering and dying on a cross. The beauty of the cross is the power of God's love to take on what is weak and fragile and transform it into the living presence of God. What Clare realizes is not only the power of God's love but the hiddenness of that love in the poor crucified Christ. God does not show power by preventing death or through force. Rather, God shows power by self-emptying love, by transforming death into life in a way invisible to the human eye and inscrutable to the human mind. Only a God of absolute love can love absolutely and transform what is dead into life.

Clare does not try to understand God's ways. She accepts the power of the cross as the power of God's love and sees in the cross the promise of happiness, joy and the riches of heaven. For Clare the victory of the crucified Christ is the triumph of love. She guides Agnes along the path of love, assuring her that God accepts what is weak as the way to reveal himself. Yet she is keenly aware that God is more than our finite earthly existence. The power of God's love is the gravity of love that can draw the human soul beyond itself to become itself, as love transforms the soul into the divine likeness. Divine likeness for Clare is the capacity to see and love another, to be "inflamed with the fervor of charity" which is the fruit of contemplation. The cross therefore is her source of hope and she is convinced that loving the crucified Christ and living in the form of crucified love will lead to the happiness of eternal life.

While Clare's depth of insight into the poverty of the crucified Christ helps us understand why the cross is central to relationship with God, her originality is in her description of the cross as a mirror. Here she sees humanity both in its greatness and in its weakness. In the mirror of the cross we see God as we see ourselves reflected in our fragile humanity. God is reflected to us, in the person of Jesus Christ, and we are reflected to ourselves. Christ crucified shows us not only the truth of our humanity but what it means to be image of God. Clare is clear that the Crucified is the image of the Godhead and the image into which we are to be transformed, as she said: "[T]ransform your entire being *into the image* / of the Godhead Itself through contemplation."[1] The cross therefore is not the place of judgment but the place of contemplation. It is not a sign of our condemnation but of our transformation into what we are created to be, the image of God. Clare's theology of the cross is liberating because it tells us that God loves us with our limitations but we are also challenged to transcend them by coming to a true acceptance of ourselves and an acceptance of others. She asks that we study who we are each day in the mirror of the cross, to look at our lives inwardly and outwardly, to recognize our dependency on others, our individuality and personality and our capacity to love. The image of Jesus on the cross reflects back to us the image of ourselves. We are to become the image of Christ crucified in our lives, not by being nailed to a cross but coming to that place of transcendent love within ourselves where we can see the suffering and recognize the charity in another. Then we are living as the image of God.

Clare's spirituality is a spiraling relationship into the loving embrace of the Trinity. Every end is a new beginning, and every arrival is a new departure, as one progresses from "good to better, from virtue to virtue."[2] The one who seeks life in God must enter into a dynamic relationship with God, a forward movement of "light steps and swift pace" that is marked by ever-deepening love and joy. Although Clare suffered physically, and probably emotionally in her lifetime, her spirituality suggests that earthly struggles are not to weigh us down in our pursuit of God. Life may have its share of difficulties but the love of God surpasses all. The way to know the love of God for Clare is through the cross. Even though we journey into God in union with the crucified Christ, the cross is not a burden to carry but a gift, although we seldom accept it with gratitude. As we take up our cross in pursuit of God, which means accepting our inequities, we are lifted up by the love of the Crucified into the embrace of God's love. To take up the cross, therefore, is to be taken up by the cross into God, an idea Clare expresses in terms of opposites: poverty/riches, time/eternity, suffering/glory, weep/rejoice, death/eternal life.[3] Thus Clare focuses on striving to love more deeply in the midst of the cross, that is, in the midst of human imperfection and suffering. For there is no human imperfection that can outweigh the power of God's love to embrace us and transform us into the beauty of the image we are created to be.

The key to Clare's theology of the cross is contemplation which is the fruit of the poor person who gazes or sees with the eye of the heart. To contemplate is to see beyond the surface, to penetrate reality and thus to dwell in love. When we can contemplate God in the crucified Christ by seeing the God of love hidden in humanity, then we can contemplate God in our crucified brothers and sisters and in the crucified human community. Because contemplation is centered in the mirror of the cross, it is not the goal of relationship with God but the way to the goal which is transformation. Clare wants us to become what we love or, rather, whom we love. As we see God hidden in the crucified Christ, so too, we are to love God. As we love God, so we are to be transformed in God. Love transforms because love unites; the lover is transformed into the beloved while remaining distinct. Clare is aware that love is born of desire, and thus she asks Agnes to desire to image Christ in her own life ("gaze on him. . .as you desire to imitate him"). Agnes must therefore progress from the poverty of the cross to the glory of transformation, letting go of everything that prevents her from becoming her true self in God. As she goes forward along this path, she will become not only rich in the love of God but transformed by this love. Ultimately the life of Agnes is to become the life of Christ in the world. Clare indicates that Christ takes on flesh anew in the life of the believer when we are free to be ourselves in God. Agnes is to study her face in the mirror of the cross, to be transformed into the image she sees, and thus to become a mirror of Christ Crucified for others to see and follow.

Clare's incarnational spirituality is radical. It is not a "consumer spirituality" for curious seekers nor is it a spirituality for the ambivalent or weak of heart. It is a spirituality of participation in the mystical Body of Christ. It is for those who want to make a personal difference in the world through personal transformation. Transformation means change. Clare calls Agnes to real change, and we might say, she calls us to change as well. Are we willing to change? What are we willing to change? Where we live or what we do for a living? Clare calls us to the root of change, to "possess" poverty as created human beings, to claim our dependency on God and our neighbor in whom God lives, to live as poor persons in relation to the poor Christ whose poverty is the wealth of love. She challenges our desires by directing them away from material things to the one thing necessary, contemplative union with God. In her own way she offers a caveat to what we desire. If we desire happiness, the reign of God, peace and justice, or if we desire that the life of Christ be the life of the world, then we must be prepared to realize these desires in our own lives. For Clare, this means living in the mirror of the cross and contemplating the image of the crucified Christ. When the life of Christ becomes the life of the believer, the life of the believer becomes the life of the church and, we might say, the life of the world. She realizes that only a crucified God can help us because only the love of the cross can transcend the limitations of our humanity and the boundaries of difference and draw together the scattered pieces of bread into the one Body of Christ. For Clare, the unity of love means we must make a personal contribution to the Body of Christ; his Body must become our bodies, his life our lives. We are not outside the Body of Christ as passive spectators; rather, we *are* the Body of Christ. We are invited into the transforming love of God because God desires to take on flesh anew in our lives. The goal of contemplation, therefore, is conversion through interior transformation and reflecting Christ in order to present the face of Christ to the world. Each of us is to be the face of Christ in the world, reflecting Christ as Christ reflects the Father. We are to live in time as if eternity has broken into our lives. We are to seek eternal life by transforming the things of time. Thus we do not seek to leave the created world but to enter into it in the form of crucified love.

As a woman who lived most of her life enclosed in a convent, Clare of Assisi had remarkable insight to the depth of the human person and the human capacity for God. She drew her insights from deep reflection on the Incarnation and the mystery of God's love in the cross, and in her day-to-day interactions with the sisters of her community. She was a woman of hope, joy, optimism and faith in the promise of God's love. Although she described her spiritual insights to a woman she never met, we are, in some way, that woman, Agnes of Prague. Each of us seeks an identity, and when we call ourselves "Christian" we not only profess an identity but we claim that identity as our own. Are we really what we claim to be when we call ourselves "Christian"? Clare challenges our identity by calling us to authentic transformation.

Interpreting Clare's spirituality for our own time can help reset the human quest for identity, meaning, purpose, and life in Christ. Clare speaks to each of these with simplicity and profundity. She asks us to take time to reflect on our lives, not in a psychological, introspective way, but in the mirror of the cross. Her thought can be summarized by saying, "see what you are, become what you love." The one who follows Christ is to bring Christ to birth in one's life,[4] and in this way to become a coworker with God. Hers is a spirituality of witness to the risen Christ. If we are transformed in the mirror of Christ we are called to radiate and manifest this image in our own lives. For Clare, transformation of the human person is the movement toward fulfillment of creation because it is participation in the Body of Christ. Her spirituality helps us understand that God will not transform the world for us but then again God will not transform the world without us. The poverty of God means that God has given everything to us in love. We are to choose that love, live in it and make it our own love. For the power of God's love is in the fragility of our lives.

NOTES

[1] Clare of Assisi, "The Third Letter to Agnes of Prague," 13 (Écrits, 102), Early Documents, p. 45.

[2] Clare of Assisi, "The First Letter to Agnes of Prague," 32 (Écrits, 90), Early Documents, p. 38.

[3] See Clare of Assisi, "The First Letter to Agnes of Prague," 19–30 (Écrits, 86–90), Early Documents, p. 37; "The Second Letter to Agnes of Prague," 20–21 (Écrits, 96–98), Early Documents, p. 42.

[4] This is Clare's idea expressed in her third letter to Agnes where she writes: "I am speaking of Him / who is the Son of the Most High / Whom the Virgin brought to birth / and remained a Virgin after His birth. /... / As the glorious Virgin of virgins carried [Him] materially, so you, too by *following in her footprints*...[can] always carry Him spiritually in your chaste and virginal body, holding Him by Whom you and *all things are held together*." (Écrits, 104–106), Early Documents, p. 46.

LIGHT

Shining in the universe,
pervading
Every corner of creation.

Invisible presence,
Uncreated essence.

Light from Light

radiating,
diffusing,
energizing

Making all things alive,
inwardly, outwardly,
uniting
all things

Together
along the galaxies of this
visible universe.

Bending back time and space,
Filling black holes
with hidden gladness.

Ready to burst forth with

energy,
goodness,
love,
New Creation

Light from Light

In whom we live and move and have our being

Diffusing through the stars
Into our hearts

Sun beams, moon beams, star beams,
All join in
the cosmic light-filled dance of praise
to the

Overflowing source of light
The Trinity
of beaming love
Spilling over with
de-light
On the lovers of creation.

Clare is among them.
She shines brilliantly

On earth her shining deeds set her apart.
On high the fullness of the divine light shines upon her.

O the wonderful brilliance of blessed Clare!

This woman grew bright in the world,
radiated in her religious life;
                shone like the sun in her home
                like a burst of lightning in the enclosure

She gave light in life;
She is radiant after death.
She was brilliant on earth,
She is resplendent in heaven!

O how great is the power of this light
And how intense is the brilliance of its illumination!

She shines on us now
Enlightens our hearts
And shows us the way

To be light
To join with her
In light

For the life of the world.

Ilia Delio, O.S.F.

BIBLIOGRAPHY

Alberzoni, Maria Pia. *Clare of Assisi and the Poor Sisters in the Thirteenth Century.* Translated by William Short and Nancy Celaschi. Saint Bonaventure, N.Y.: Franciscan Institute, 2004.

Armstrong, Regis J. *St. Francis of Assisi: Writings for a Gospel Life.* New York: Crossroad, 1994.

Bartoli, Marco. *Clare of Assisi.* Translated by Sister Frances Teresa. Quincy, Ill.: Franciscan Press, 1993.

Carney, Margaret. *The First Franciscan Woman: Clare of Assisi and Her Form of Life.* Quincy, Ill.: Franciscan Press, 1994.

Clare of Assisi: Early Documents. Edited and translated by Regis J. Armstrong. Saint Bonaventure, N.Y.: Franciscan Institute, 1993.

Costello, Liam Francis. *Through the Veils of Morning: An Inner Journey in the Pathways of Francis and Clare of Assisi.* Skokie, Ill.: ACTA, 2000.

Delio, Ilia. *Simply Bonaventure: An Introduction to his Life, Thought, and Writings.* New York: New City Press, 2001.

Francis of Assisi: Early Documents. Volume I. *The Saint.* Edited by Regis J. Armstrong, J.A. Wayne Hellmann, and William J. Short. New York: New City Press, 1999.

Francis of Assisi: Early Documents. Volume II. *The Founder.* Edited by Regis J. Armstrong, J.A. Wayne Hellmann, and William J. Short. New York: New City Press, 2000.

Godet-Calogeras, Jean François and Roberta McKelvie (eds.). *An Unencumbered Heart: A Tribute to Clare of Assisi, 1253–2003.* Saint Bonaventure, N.Y.: Franciscan Institute, 2004.

Haase, Albert. *Swimming in the Sun: Discovering the Lord's Prayer with Francis of Assisi and Thomas Merton.* Cincinnati: St. Anthony Messenger Press, 1993.

Himes, Michael and Kenneth. *Fullness of Faith: The Public Significance of Theology.* New York: Paulist, 1993.

Hone, Mary Francis (ed.). *Towards the Discovery of Clare of Assisi.* Translated by Regis J. Armstrong and Pacelli Millane. Saint Bonaventure, N.Y.: Franciscan Institute, 1992.

Llull, Ramon. *The Book of the Lover and the Beloved.* Translated by Mark D. Johnston. Warminster: Aris and Phillips, 1995.

Merton, Thomas. *New Seeds of Contemplation.* New York: New Directions, 1961.

Panikkar, Raimon, *Christophany: The Fullness of Man.* Translated by Alfred DiLascia. Maryknoll, N.Y.: Orbis, 2004.

Peterson, Ingrid J. *Clare of Assisi: A Biographical Study.* Quincy, Ill.: Franciscan Press, 1993.

Petroff, Elizabeth A. *Consolation of the Blessed.* New York: Alta Gaia Society, 1979.

Sister Frances Teresa. *This Living Mirror: Reflections on Clare of Assisi.* Maryknoll, N.Y.: Orbis, 1995.

The Works of Bonaventure: Cardinal, Seraphic Doctor, and Saint. 5 Volumes. Translated by José de Vinck. Paterson, N.J.: St. Anthony Guild Press, 1960–1970.

Van den Goorbergh, Edith and Theodore H. Zweerman. *Light Shining Through a Veil.* Translated by Sister Frances Teresa. Leuven: Peeters, 2000.

Volf, Miroslav. *Exclusion and Embrace: A Theological Exploration of Identity, Otherness, and Reconciliation.* Nashville: Abingdon, 1996.

INDEX

poverty and, 23
humans
call to sanctity, 109
dependence upon God, 33, 37
face, and identity, 42
identity, 42-44, 46-47, 117-118
as image of God, 38, 102
poverty and, 10
relationship to God, 8
selfishness and, 31
See also Jesus, humanity of

Incarnation, 24
Clare's view of, 116-117
See also Jesus, humanity of
Innocent III, Pope, xi
Innocent IV, Pope, xvi

Jesus
as "beloved Spouse," 3
crucified, 30, 31, 83. See also
San Damiano, cross of
humanity of, 3, 7, 35
as image of God, 28
imitation of, ix
poverty of, 19
as priest, 34
John, Saint
Gospel of, 34, 104

La Verna, 75, 107, 108
Last Supper, 34
Leo, Brother, xviii
Llull, Ramon, 10-11

Major Legend of Saint Francis,
(Bonaventure), 15, 107
Mary
as Theotokos, 78
Matthew, Saint
Gospel of, xix
kingdom theology of, xix
Meister Eckhart. See Eckhart,
Meister
Merton, Thomas, 13, 46
mirror (symbol)
Agnes of Prague and, 29
cross as, 26, 29, 33, 36, 48
in Middle Ages, 26
Paul on, 27
"mirror mystic," 26
monastic ascent
Neoplatonic structure of, xiii
Montaldo (Clare's uncle), xii

Neoplatonism, xiii

obedience, 22. See also entry under
Clare
Old Testament, 28

Panikkar, Raimon, 103, 104,
105, 110
Panzo, xii
Paul, Saint, 21, 27
eucharistic theology, 81
on flesh, 83
Poor Ladies, xiv
Portiuncola, xi, xii, xvii
poverty

SCRIPTURE INDEX